SENTINEL

AMERICAN DREAMS

Marco Rubio served in the Florida House of Representatives from 2000 to 2008 and was elected Speaker of the House in 2006. In 2010, he was elected to the U.S. Senate. His first book, *An American Son*, was a *New York Times* bestseller. He and his wife, Jeanette, have four young children and live in West Miami.

AMERICAN DREAMS

RESTORING ECONOMIC
OPPORTUNITY FOR EVERYONE

Marco Rubio

SENTINEL

SENTINEL
An imprint of Penguin Random House LLC
375 Hudson Street
New York, New York 10014
penguin.com

First published in the United States of America by Sentinel, an imprint of Penguin Random House LLC, 2015
This paperback edition with a new epilogue published 2015

THE LIBRARY OF CONGRESS HAS CATALOGED THE HARDCOVER EDITION AS FOLLOWS:
Rubio, Marco, 1971-
American dreams: restoring economic opportunity for everyone / Marco Rubio.
pages cm
Includes bibliographical references and index.
ISBN 978-1-59523-113-0 (hc.)
ISBN 978-0-14-310903-7 (pbk.)
1. United States—Economic policy—2009- 2. United States—Economic conditions—2009- 3. United States—Social policy—2009- 4. United States—Politics and government—2009- 5. Middle class—United States. I. Title.
HC106.84.R83 2015
330.973—dc23   2014038671

Printed in the United States of America
10 9 8 7 6 5 4 3 2 1

Set in Adobe Garamond Pro
Designed by Daniel Lagin

To the American Dream
and all who are pursuing it.

Contents

CONTENTS

Introduction

RESTORING THE AMERICAN DREAM

My grandfather Pedro Víctor García was born in rural Cuba in the last year of the nineteenth century. He was stricken with polio at a young age, which left him permanently disabled. Since he was unable to work on the family farm, his parents sent him away to school because it was the only way he would ever have a chance to support himself when he grew up. He learned to read and write quite well, a skill that got him hired as a lector, reading newspapers and novels to workers at a cigar factory. He also learned to be a telegraph operator, a skill that would one day land him a job with a railroad company.

In time, though, he lost his job at the railroad to a politically connected coworker. After that, he struggled to provide for his seven daughters. My mother remembers how he spent all day looking for odd jobs—not easy for a disabled man in a developing country. He would return home in the evenings with bleeding cuts and scrapes on his legs because his limp had caused him to slip and fall throughout the day. Ultimately, he ended up repairing shoes in Havana before coming to America.

Papá, as we called him, lived with us for most of the first thirteen years of my life. Every day he would put on a suit and tie and sit outside on a folding aluminum lawn chair to smoke one of his three daily cigars. I spent hours sitting with him, listening to him share his stories about history, politics and baseball. I could always count on him to feed my curiosity about history, ranging from World War II to Cuban independence. Looking back now, I realize that the greatest impact Papá had on me was a simple and powerful lesson embedded in all of our talks.

When he was young, he had big dreams and ambitions for himself. He had an interest in politics and world affairs, as well as the gift of communication. He wanted to put those talents to use as a leader of industry or state. But he was disabled. He wasn't politically connected. And his family had no wealth. So, as with most people in the world, his future was determined more by the circumstances of his birth than by his dreams or his ability.

Papá wanted me to know that my life could be different. Unlike him, I would have the chance to go as far as my talent and my work would take me. I was a citizen of the one place on earth where even the son of a bartender and a maid could grow up to achieve any dream. I was an American.

It is easy for those of us who were born and have lived our entire lives in the United States to fail to appreciate how unique our country is. But people like my grandfather knew. And if we listen, they remind us of something important.

Over two centuries ago, a nation was founded on the belief

that all people had a God-given right to life, liberty and the pursuit of happiness. From then on, the world would never be the same again. Our founders put in place a republic and a free-enterprise economy designed to promote and protect this God-given right. And the result was the single greatest nation in all of human history.

Papá split his time between Miami and Las Vegas, where we lived for a few years during my childhood. By the summer of 1984, he knew he was nearing the end of his life, so he decided to cut his time in Miami short and come home to us. In August, he fell and broke his hip. My mother asked me to ride in the ambulance with him to the hospital so I could help him communicate with the paramedics. I remember standing in the hallway outside the X-ray room and hearing him groan in pain as they tried to take X-rays of his broken hip. And I remember standing by his bedside the next day as he began to slip into a coma in the last hours of his life.

As he slipped away, I held his hand and I made him a promise: I was going to study. I was going to make something of myself. I would not waste the opportunity I had to achieve my dreams. And he squeezed my hand as if to let me know he was at peace.

Every day since that day I have worked to make good on my promise to my grandfather. Like everyone, I've made mistakes and I've fallen short. But, thanks to him, to my parents, and to the promise of the country they adopted as their own, I have been able to realize his dream for me. I have a wife and family that I love. I am privileged to represent the people of Florida in the U.S. Senate. My life is blessed.

What bothers me most about my country today is that there

are Americans like me—Americans who have worked hard and tried to do the right things to get ahead—but whose lives aren't so blessed. Jennifer, a young woman in her twenties who lives in Miami, is such an American, an heir to the American Dream just as I am. But her life has not worked out as planned—at least not so far. She has done everything right. She has played by the rules. But she hasn't achieved her American Dream. She's starting to doubt she ever will.

When Jennifer was growing up, her father always told her that an education was the key to a life better than his own. She took him at his word, worked hard and went to Florida International University. Four years ago, she graduated with a degree in public administration. She was the first in her family to go to college. Despite having paid for what she thought was the ticket to a better life, Jennifer has begun to wonder whether college was a waste of her time and money. The only job she can find has nothing to do with her degree. Her salary is barely enough to cover her monthly bills, let alone put anything aside to save for a house of her own. To make matters worse, her father recently got laid off. And because she doesn't make enough to help him out, they've had to do what too many other Americans have had to do: form a "multigenerational housing unit." In other words, they've moved in with Jennifer's grandmother.

A generation ago, Jennifer's current wage might have been enough for her to reach the middle class. But today, her monthly expenses are prohibitive: $300 for her car payment, $200 for car insurance, $200 for gas, $200 for food, $100 for her cell phone bill—just to name a few. She'd like to go back to school to earn a graduate degree, but she doesn't want the $50,000 in debt she would incur. She has none of the confidence, held by earlier generations of Americans, that investing in herself through education will pay off in the job market.

Like me, Jennifer grew up in a country that has always prided itself on offering an equal opportunity for its people to get ahead— not a guarantee of equal success, but of an equal opportunity to go as far as your hard work and your wits can take you. People everywhere dream of better lives for themselves and for their children, of course. Yet for the vast majority of humanity, and for the vast majority of history, this simply wasn't possible. As my grandfather never let me forget, though, it is different in America. Here, so many people from humble or disadvantaged backgrounds have achieved their ambitions that this universal hope has been given a name. It has come to be known as the American Dream.

The American Dream still lives. But it is slipping further and further out of reach of millions of Americans, and this is the central challenge of our time. How we respond to this challenge— and whether we are successful—will determine whether we continue to be an exceptional nation.

For conservatives especially, this is a defining moment. The failure of government-centered, command-and-control liberalism to lift the poor and sustain the middle class is apparent as never before. Whether we are able to step forward with our own solutions—and not simply rail against the expansion of the state— will determine our future as a movement.

Our recent history in this regard is not encouraging. President Barack Obama was elected on a promise to fight for poor and middle-class Americans like Jennifer. During his campaigns for president, he talked directly to the American people about the girl who's worried she can't go to college because she can't afford it, about the dad who doesn't know if his wages will cover the winter heating bill, about the single mom who's stressed about what her children are doing after school while she's at work. Meanwhile, my party talked about tax cuts and waited for the American people to punish the president for the economy. They didn't. He won. We lost.

And yet seven years into his presidency, struggling Americans are—by every measure—worse off today than they were before he took office. Why has a president elected as a champion of the disadvantaged failed so miserably at helping them? Because, like most liberals, he doesn't understand the real causes of the erosion of equal opportunity we are experiencing today. He has raised taxes, increased regulations and taken over health care—all according to the outdated liberal theory that Americans struggle when government doesn't tax the rich enough and spend on the poor enough. But the results, such as they are, speak for themselves. After seven years of old-school liberalism, fewer Americans are working than at any time since Jimmy Carter, new business creation is 30 percent lower than it was in the 1980s and the economy shrank by the highest rate since the Great Recession in the first quarter of 2014.

It's getting harder for millions of Americans to get ahead, not because our taxes are too low or our government is too stingy. The poor and the middle class are struggling because while our economy is undergoing a dramatic and disruptive transformation, our policies have not changed with it. Our economy is no longer producing enough well-paying jobs, not enough people have the skills they need for better-paying jobs and the values needed for success are eroding at an alarming rate.

The rise of dozens of developed economies means we have more competition for jobs than ever before. Yet our tax code makes it more expensive to invest in America in comparison to our competition. Rapid advances in technology and the globalization of the economy have meant that many of the jobs that once made the American Dream possible are now being outsourced or automated. Overall, our regulations are causing us to lose our advantage in innovation.

Many of our low-skill jobs once paid enough to make it to the middle class. But now many of them pay wages that have not kept up with the cost of living. Today's better-paying jobs require higher education or skills training, but we have an outdated, expensive, inaccessible education system that fails to graduate students with skills that prepare them for work. Older students who have to work full-time and raise a family struggle to access a higher education system that wasn't built for them. And a college education has become more expensive than ever, leaving millions of young Americans with massive student loans.

Underlying these economic changes are societal ones. To succeed in life, you don't just need skills and a good job. You need to have values like hard work, discipline and self-control. No one is born with these values. They have to be taught by families and faith. But today, we face a serious erosion of family life in America. Millions of children are growing up in unstable homes in which they are not taught the values necessary for personal and economic success.

The result is a pervasive—and growing—sense of insecurity. Instead of adjusting to the realities of the new era, however, our leaders are doubling down on policies and institutions designed in the middle of the last century. Our taxes, our schools, our regulations, our immigration system and our poverty and retirement programs—they're all relics of the last century. They were conceived and created at a time when America faced limited international competition, at a time when, even with no formal education, you could find a low-skill job that paid a middle-class wage. But this is not the world we live in anymore.

Failing to adjust to the realities of a new era is a recurring theme in history. We don't want to be the generals who are busy fighting the last war. During World War II, the U.S. Army's last chief of the cavalry, Major General John Herr, was asked to develop a plan to confront and defeat the German Panzers. He concluded that the cavalry horses were failing to stop the German tanks because they were too tired after a long journey to the front. Herr's brilliant insight was to use tractor trailers to move the horses closer to the battlefield so they would be better rested and thus able to defeat the Panzers. Fortunately for America and the world, General George Marshall's response to this plan was to retire General Herr, get rid of the horses and reorganize the army.

General Herr's kind of thinking is exactly what is wrong with our politics today. Liberals want to spend more money on the ideas of yesterday. Some conservatives want to keep the ideas of yesterday and just spend less on them, as if programs that aren't working will somehow be made to function if only their budgets are cut. But neither of these approaches will ever work. No matter how much we spent on those horses or how efficient we made them, they were never going to stop those tanks. And no matter how much we spend on the ideas of the last century, or how much we streamline some of them, they are never going to help us reclaim the American Dream for all.

America needs leaders who understand the new world we live in and who will promote and implement new ideas for a new era. We can't solve our twenty-first-century challenges by simply investing more into twentieth-century solutions. And yet this is precisely what those who would succeed President Obama show every intention of doing.

On each of the major challenges facing America, for example, Hillary Clinton has proven herself wedded to the policies and programs of the past. Instead of reforming a higher education system that costs too much money, is too hard for nontraditional students to access and awards too many degrees that do not lead to jobs, another Clinton presidency will be about spending more money on a broken system. Instead of cutting back on regulations that stifle innovation and deny consumer choice, another Clinton presidency will be about enacting regulations her friends in the corporate world use to prevent competition. Instead of reforming an anticompetitive tax code that has made America one of the most expensive places on earth to invest and create jobs, another Clinton presidency will be about raising taxes to pay for a growing government. The election of Hillary Clinton to the presidency, in short, would be nothing more than a third Obama term. Another Clinton presidency would be a death blow to the American Dream.

For our part, conservatives have also failed to address the challenges of the new economy—but there are promising signs that this is changing. As the opposition party, we have typically responded to attempts to build an ever bigger, ever more intrusive government by calling for less government and less spending. These are essential and nonnegotiable goals for conservatism. But, as conservative writer and editor Yuval Levin has pointed out, absent a broader governing agenda, this response leaves the impression that all conservatives care about is a less expensive welfare state, one that costs fewer of the 1 percent's tax dollars. This response neatly sets up a debate that the left is all too happy for the American people to hear: liberals, who care about people like you, versus conservatives, who don't.

To their credit, Levin and other thinkers and policy makers on the right—particularly those at the American Enterprise Institute—have begun to move conservatives away from fixating on what we are against and instead toward thinking about what we are for. It is difficult work. America's economic and cultural problems are serious and complex. But conservatives come to this effort with a distinct advantage: We are not the party of government. We are not the party wedded to the status quo ideas and the Washington interest groups that are failing Americans today. We don't need to abandon our faith in free enterprise, federalism and limited government to find solutions for middle-class Americans. In fact, our principles are the necessary supports for such an agenda. We need only to find innovative and creative ways to apply these principles to real people's lives.

The American Dream may not survive another four years of outdated, status quo leadership. America is in dire need of a new direction, a true break with the ineffectual liberal policies of the last century. We need a clear vision forward that puts opportunity over cronyism, work over dependency and the health of the American family over all. America needs a conservative reform agenda.

This book is my attempt to construct such an agenda, told through the voices of the real people most in need of help today. Through the stories of an ambitious small-business man, a struggling single mother, an out-of-work and in-debt college graduate, among others, I focus on the three central elements to the achievement of the American Dream: equal opportunity, economic security and family. These are the American virtues that have always defined the dream, and they are the ones most threatened today. Americans believe, with increasing reason, that the equal opportunity to work and to succeed that our nation has always promised has been lost in a system rigged to favor the wealthy and well connected. Economic security, which used to be possible to achieve through a high school education and hard work, is no longer within reach of many families. And the family itself—always both the means and the ends of the American Dream—is struggling as never before.

Now is not the time to downgrade the American Dream. Now is the time to rescue it. Despite the hard times so many American families are experiencing, there is reason for great optimism. America is still the place my parents were drawn to in 1956; it is still a country where people can achieve their dreams. We can restore the American Dream and expand it to reach more people than ever before. But to do so, we must set out a new direction that gives us a government with less debt and less power, an economy with more stable middle-class jobs, and families healthy and secure enough to achieve their dreams.

The challenges before us are formidable, but before we start feeling sorry for ourselves, we need to remember the sacrifices that brought us to this point. Every generation of Americans before us has been asked to take bold and difficult steps to preserve what makes us special. Reforming our entitlements will be difficult, yes. But does it really compare with defeating the Nazis or eliminating Jim Crow? Imagine if our parents and grandparents hadn't risen to those challenges. Think about how different our lives would be.

When I was in college and then later in law school, my parents wanted me to focus on my studies. They didn't want me working and going to school part-time. So I lived at home. My father worked as a bartender well into his seventies, long past the time he should have retired. Many of the banquets he worked were on Friday and Saturday nights. So many late nights I recall hearing the jingle of his keys at the door, well past midnight, as he returned from another ten-hour day at work.

I didn't fully appreciate it then, but I know now that the sound at the door wasn't just the sound of keys. It was the sound of the unfulfilled dreams of my father's youth. It was the sound of a father whose entire life was now about making sure I would never have to go through what he went through. It was the sound of his American Dream.

This story is not mine alone. It is the story of a young mother who dreams of something better for her daughters. It is the story of small-business owners struggling to survive in a system rigged against them. It is the story of a young woman who rises from homelessness and abuse to become a teacher.

Hearing their stories has given me a sobering glimpse of the human toll that our failed response to the changed economy is having on American families. But it has also given me hope. It has convinced me that, despite our many differences, we are more united than our politics would lead you to believe. We are all the descendants of immigrants and slaves who refused to accept the limits of the Old World. They were men and women who took great risks and paid a great price to earn a better life. This is who we come from. Their blood runs in our veins.

No one book, no one man or woman, can restore the American Dream. But a movement, focusing its principles on creative and innovative solutions for American families, can provide the starting point. And a people, eager to be more than wards of government—eager to achieve their own American Dreams—can turn those solutions into realities.

I believe deeply in the conservative reform proposals presented in these pages. But what they seek to achieve—a rising, striving America for all of us—isn't partisan. There isn't a Republican Dream and a Democratic Dream. There is only one American Dream. Before us lies the chance not just to restore it, but to bring it within reach of more people than ever before. This is our chance to claim our heritage as a people who always leave behind a nation better than the one left to them.

My grandparents and parents kept the dream alive. So did yours. Now it's our turn.

AMERICAN DREAMS

Chapter One

THE AMERICAN DREAM, DOWNSIZED

Jose's dad used to tell him, "You don't drown by falling in water. You drown by staying in water." So when his accountant embezzled from his architecture business he didn't dwell on the fact that he was the victim of a crime. He didn't seek revenge. The accountant was a mother of three—three kids who needed her— so Jose didn't press for jail time. He just wanted restitution.

The court awarded him that restitution, but when the recession hit and Jose's firm went under, he faced his employees and took responsibility for the failure. The buck stopped with him. When you talk to him about it today, he tells you, unbidden, that he wishes he saw more of that in Washington.

At forty-one, he has lost his business, and with a wife and two kids to support, Jose has had to start his life over again. He's had to go back to school to get his master's degree, which he hopes will give him an edge in a competitive market. At the same time, he works full-time, leads the Boy Scout troop at his church and worries about the burden that puts on his wife, Lisa, who manages to work part-time while taking point with their eleven-year-old son and nine-year-old daughter.

Adding to his troubles is the fact that grad school is expensive. A residential program, where he would sit in a classroom with other students, was out of the question. Jose managed to find a more affordable program—one of the few distance learning master's in architecture programs in the country—out of state. He takes his classes online, but once a month he has to travel 1,750 miles round-trip to meet with his professors. He estimates he already owes $50,000 to $60,000 in student loans and he has no idea how he's going to pay them off, but he wants more for his family, so he'll find a way.

Jose and Lisa are living, breathing refutations of one of the most unfortunate ideas to gain currency recently: the notion that Americans have somehow changed, that there is now a large number of us who would rather depend on government than work.

This simply isn't true. Of course, there will always be some who would rather get a handout than a hand up. But the vast majority of Americans, like Jose and Lisa, are willing to do whatever it takes to get ahead. The flip side of that argument, however, is equally offensive. It's the idea that if you're successful—even if you're just ambitious—you don't have yourself and your hard work to thank; you have government to thank. Perhaps the most famous articulation of this view came in the summer before the 2012 election, when President Obama told a campaign audience in Virginia, "If you've got a business, you didn't build that."

Government can play a role in our success, of course. The rule of law, infrastructure, access to quality education and a pro-growth tax and regulatory code help create the environment for prosperity. This is the proper and important role of government in making free enterprise work. But what President Obama, Hillary Clinton and other liberals believe goes well beyond this limited role. They believe that government doesn't just create the environment for prosperity; they believe it is its primary driver. And they believe that the one thing struggling Americans need or want most is a government check.

In this view, the government safety net isn't a temporary bridge to a better life but a permanent way of life. Politically, this can be a compelling agenda. When people lament the quality of our schools, it can be an effective talking point to say how much you want to spend on education, as opposed to empowering parents with more choices. And when the struggles of people like Jose and Lisa come up, it can be a rewarding position during an election to propose to spend money to lower interest rates on student loans or to offer government-subsidized health insurance, rather than encourage innovation and competition to bring prices down.

The problem with this approach, however, is that in the end it just makes Americans feel better while they're clinging to a lower rung of the economic ladder. It doesn't help them rise. Like a record number of Americans during the Obama presidency, Lisa and Jose considered government assistance when the recession hit and their business failed. For a while, they weren't sure they were going to be able to keep their house. Jose is grateful the help is available. But what he really wants is to get his degree and be able to provide for himself and his family. He is frustrated that the assistance he gets doesn't help him do that. What's more, he sees government tipping the scales *against* his success. He used to dream of starting his own business again after getting his degree, but these days he's not so sure.

"The truth is, right now I am very cautious about embarking on that journey again," says Jose. "I don't believe that the rules are on my side to succeed." A few years after his business failed, he and Lisa tried to start another business, but the cost of insurance and benefits forced them to, as he says, "1099" their employees—bring them on as independent contractors, without tax withholding or benefits. Since then, the prospects for businesspeople like Jose and Lisa have only gotten worse.

The regulations placed on small-business owners have grown so burdensome that Jose now finds himself tempted by the idea that he might be better off working for someone else for the rest of his life rather than try to build something of his own. "I have no idea what's being mandated or what problems we could run into," he says. "How can anybody move forward with blind faith?"

Among the challenges people like Jose now face are the realities of a new economy that is fundamentally different from the one his parents—and my parents—encountered when they came to America decades ago. The opportunity to better yourself no matter who you are is something that has appealed to Jose about America since he came here as a child. But now, like too many Americans, Jose feels that, even though he is working hard, that sense of limitless opportunity is slipping away. "The American Dream is kids doing better than their parents," he says. "I look around and I really feel like we're going backwards."

Americans still want to work, achieve and get ahead. Liberals have failed to adequately appreciate this, and conservatives have failed to adequately support it. What America needs now is a conservative movement that understands the challenges people like Jose and Lisa face, and offers bold and relevant ideas to help them thrive in a changed economy.

The America my parents came to in 1956 was a place where it was possible for two people with grade school educations and jobs in the service sector to have a car, buy a home and send their kids to college. As a maid and a bartender, my parents did all these things. The world was recovering from World War II and America was unchallenged in its manufacturing and economic strength. The period from the late 1940s through the early 1970s saw the mean family income double for the rich, the middle class and the poor.[1] Veterans were returning from war and going to college on the GI Bill. Whether they went to college or not, Americans were getting jobs in expanding industries, buying homes and going to Miami on vacation. My family and I were the beneficiaries.

Today, those years of growth and shared prosperity seem like ancient history. Something has happened to the American economy and the American Dream that goes beyond the usual boom and bust, recession and recovery of the business cycle. Something structural has shifted—something that is upending the lives and diminishing the futures of millions.

After decades of growing incomes for the middle class, the years between 2000 and 2011 were what the Pew Research Center calls a "lost decade." In those years, middle-class Americans made less money, had more debt and had less wealth—in fact, for the first time since World War II, the middle class actually shrank in size. Median income fell by 5 percent and median wealth—the amount of a family's assets minus their debt—dropped a tragic 28 percent. For the poorest Americans, net worth plunged an astounding 48 percent.[2]

For most Americans, wages are stagnant. Old jobs have been outsourced or automated. The jobs that are available have changed, and the skills needed to fill those jobs have changed. Middle-class Americans are living paycheck to paycheck, juggling bill payments to stay one step ahead of debt collection agencies. Saving for retirement is barely manageable; saving for college is impossible.

Some call it the "hollowing out of the middle class." Others call it the "income gap." Whatever you call it, the number of American families who can call themselves middle class is shrinking as the jobs, the skills and the habits that are the keys to the American Dream have shrunk as well. And at the same time the middle class has been shrinking, the share of Americans at either end of the income spectrum—the high earners and the low earners—has grown.

Almost nine million jobs were lost during the recession, and of those, a full 60 percent were middle-class jobs in occupations like construction, manufacturing, insurance, real estate and information technology. The jobs that have come back since the recession officially ended, in contrast, are overwhelmingly in low-wage occupations. A full 58 percent of the newly created jobs pay less than around $13.50 an hour.[3] The new jobs are in areas such as food service and retail sales, personal and home care aides, laborers and freight workers. The result is that the period *after* the official end of the recession in June 2009 has been *worse* for the wages of American workers than the actual recession. The wages of the typical worker fell more than twice as much between June 2009 and June 2011 than they did during the recession—6.7 percent compared with 3.2 percent. Add it all up and median income in 2011 was 8 percent lower than in 2007.[4]

Even more frightening is the record decline in the number of Americans who are working at all. Participation in the labor force is so low today that the traditional unemployment rate is irrelevant because it counts only people who are looking for work—it doesn't account for the growing number of people who have simply given up on work altogether. Since 2008, according to the American Enterprise Institute's Nicholas Eberstadt, there has been "an obvious and almost total disconnect between the U.S. unemployment rate and the nation's work rate." In May 2014, five years into the "recovery," the percentage of Americans actually working or looking for a job had declined to 62.8 percent—the lowest level since 1979.[5] Most troublesome of all is that this decline of work is pronounced among men of prime working age. For every man between twenty-five and fifty-four who is looking for a job today, there are two who reportedly are not even looking.[6]

Americans can and do argue about the reasons for the decline of work and the disappearance of good middle-class jobs. What is beyond dispute, however, is that the policies that have been put in place since the recession have done nothing to stop these disturbing trends and in some cases have made them worse. America has had recessions and depressions before, and our average recovery time has been around thirty-three months. Yet, as of November 2014, our "recovery" stood at sixty-five months—and counting. And the long-term projections for our economy don't give us any reason for hope.

Economists calculate something called the potential gross domestic product—the total amount of goods and services our economy would produce if it were operating at full employment without inflation, using all its resources and available labor. In 2014 the Congressional Budget Office (CBO) revised—down—its estimate for our projected gross domestic product in 2017. Our best economists now believe that our economic output in two years will be 8.1 percent *less* than they initially thought it would be. That translates into a loss of $1.45 trillion in economic growth.

Taken together, these trends of declining jobs, declining work and declining economic growth amount to what some are calling the "new normal." Previous economic downturns have been followed by robust recoveries that have lifted the middle class. Why isn't the same thing happening now? What is different about this time? And why, if we stay on the current course, does it appear our current troubles will become our new normal? The answer is that our current challenges are not being driven by a cyclical economic downturn. They are being driven by a dramatic restructuring and transformation of our economy. But our policies have not been restructured and transformed to address it.

The blame for this failure belongs to both parties in Washington D.C. Republicans haven't been creative or innovative enough in offering solutions. We have spent plenty of time opposing the

president's agenda, but not nearly enough time applying our principles of limited government and free enterprise to the challenges
of our time. Until just recently, not enough Republicans have
focused on how a limited government could play a role in supporting the things we believe in—things like work, competition
and family.

And while Republicans have been guilty of the sin of omission,
Democrats are guilty of the sin of commission. To ease the pain of
the new normal, they simply offer Americans more government
programs in an attempt to compensate for lost wages and missed
opportunity. This approach implies that a lack of work, high unemployment and low economic growth are here to stay. Under the
Democrats' plan, Americans should sit back and accept diminished
lives and diminished freedom in exchange for government-granted
security.

Such has been the story of the Obama presidency. In 2008,
Barack Obama ran as a committed centrist—a twenty-first-
century leader who would unite our country to confront and solve
the new problems of a new era. But almost immediately upon
taking office, he was unmasked as an old-fashioned big-government
liberal. Tellingly, he and other Democratic leaders chose to put at
the center of their agenda the income inequality between the rich
and the nonrich. The message to working- and middle-class Americans was unmistakable: The reason for your lack of mobility
somehow lies in the fortunes of others. The success of the wealthy,
they told us, accounts for the lack of good jobs, the stagnant wages
and the growing cost of living for everyone else. The result is that,
for over six years now, the president and his ideological allies have

pursued policies—from health care to energy—to redistribute wealth rather than grow it for all.

But government, which has been expanded in the name of the poor and the middle class—Americans like Jose—has only diminished their opportunity to get ahead. For example, government regulations and mandates in the Affordable Care Act have created too much uncertainty to risk starting a new business. Both the legislation and the rhetoric coming out of Washington are making Jose and millions like him feel that going into business today is only for those who can afford to hire the army of lawyers and accountants it now takes to simply follow all the laws. That is why he has concluded that the smartest thing he can do now, he says, is "just wait and see."

"Nancy Pelosi said it," Jose says. " 'We have to pass the bill to find out what's in it.' If she's going to take that attitude—if our leaders are going to take that attitude—why would they expect the citizens to do any different?"

Government doesn't have to be the enemy, but too much government has produced a new kind of inequality in America: opportunity inequality. This is the inequality between those who can afford to influence government and those, like Jose, who can't. Income inequality—so much the focus of liberals these days—is a by-product of opportunity inequality. After six years in which those most hurt by the economic downturn have fallen further behind, it is time we acknowledge how government overreach is reducing opportunity and threatening the American Dream.

Big government has always been an impediment to upward mobility, and this is truer than ever in the new economy of the twenty-first century. We no longer have simply a national economy; we are all participants in a global economy. Things happening on the other side of the world can have a larger impact on our lives than things happening on the other side of town. In a global economy, it's become easier and more cost effective for the jobs in manufacturing, customer service and computer support that used to be done by Americans to be done in India or the Philippines.

Whether we like it or not, globalization is real and it is here to stay. Our challenge now is to position ourselves to take advantage of the opportunities it presents us, not simply suffer from the disruptions it creates. We hear a lot about global competitiveness, but the challenge we face is much more than just a race for power or national bragging rights. We are in competition with other nations for the investment, innovation and talent that will create good, well-paying jobs. The health of the middle class is at stake.

The reason big government fails now more than ever is that it makes it harder for us to win this competition. If we want to restore the American Dream, we need tax policies, regulatory policies and spending policies that make America the best place in the world to invest, and the easiest place in the world to create new businesses and new jobs through innovation. Instead, big government gives us tax policies, regulatory policies and spending policies that are making America a more expensive and burdensome place to invest and innovate.

Another culprit economists increasingly point to for the changing economy is technology. For most of the years after World

War II—including when I was growing up—new technologies *added* to the productivity of American workers, helping us produce more and faster. But today's advances in artificial intelligence and robotics aren't always helping American workers. In many cases they're *replacing* them. I don't buy into the dystopian scenarios of self-aware robots enslaving mankind, but you don't have to be a sci-fi conspiracy theorist to acknowledge that plenty of good, well-paying jobs are being taken over by machines. All you have to do is go through the self-checkout line at the supermarket, or ask UPS workers nervously eyeing Amazon's plans to replace them with delivery drones.

Just like globalization, technology is here to stay, and our challenge is to find the opportunities it presents and to take advantage of them. These technological breakthroughs aren't all bad news for the middle class. Even as machines take over more functions in our modern economy, we will still need humans to build them, fix them and work alongside them.

The key to using new technology to our advantage is having educational and vocational training systems that produce workers capable of working with it. In his book *Average Is Over*, economist Tyler Cowen sees a future in which high earners are those who "get" computers and information technology. Low earners, he argues, will be those who don't—the less technologically adept who will be forced to work in jobs attending to the needs and wants of the high earners.

Cowen concedes that you won't have to be a future Steve Jobs or even a computer programmer to be among the high earners, just someone prepared to work with technology to solve real-world problems or fill real-world needs. He points to the fact, for example, that Facebook founder and zillionaire Mark Zuckerberg was a psychology major, not a computer science major. Zuckerberg didn't know how computers work, but he understood how they could be used to fill a human need.

Cowen's vision of the future is very interesting but ultimately, I think, pessimistic. He puts the split between the high-earning winners and the low-earning losers in the coming high-tech economy at 15 to 85. There's no question that technology is changing and will continue to change American jobs. But I am certain we can do better than a future in which only 15 percent of us adapt to working with that technology.

Here, again, big government is making it harder for Americans to acquire the skills they need to benefit from the opportunities created by technology. Our current system of education, from kindergarten through graduate school, was designed in the middle of the twentieth century. That is, it was designed for an era in which we had plenty of low-skill jobs that paid middle-class incomes, a time when higher education was an option, and our higher education students were primarily recent high school graduates.

In the twenty-first century, there is a rapidly shrinking pool of middle-income jobs for low-skill workers. Education is no longer an option—it is a necessity—but our system is failing to prepare Americans for the jobs of the new economy. A recent international study showed the United States falling dangerously far behind other countries—such as Japan, Sweden and Chile—when it comes to promoting the skills needed to compete in the modern workforce. We're only average in literacy and problem-solving skills compared with most of the countries we compete with. And when it comes to math skills—the skill most prized in today's new economy—we're bringing up the rear. Only Italy's and Spain's workers performed worse than ours in math. And worse yet, while other countries seem to be racing to catch up, our skills gap is deepening. While younger workers in other countries consistently scored higher on skills tests than the generations that came before them, our thirty-year-olds actually scored lower on literacy in 2012 than thirty-year-olds in 1994 did.[7]

Big government is failing Americans because, instead of promoting transformational reforms to our education system, our leaders just want to spend more money on the status quo. This is true in higher education, where instead of creating the space for innovative and affordable higher education programs, the system seeks to shield itself from competition and innovation.

It's especially true in primary and secondary education. When Democratic politicians at all levels of government actively oppose strengthening our schools through competition and parental choice, they are hurting the very people they claim to care about most—and at a time when education is more important to achieving the American Dream than ever before.

In New York City, for example, Mayor Bill de Blasio has declared open season on publicly funded charter schools. Rich families can afford to send their children to virtually any school they choose. But by forcing poor families to send their children to failing and stagnant schools, Mayor De Blasio is making those who need the most help less able to compete for the middle-class jobs of the future. The fact that these are the very same politicians who spend their time decrying income inequality only adds insult to the injury they are inflicting on Americans.

There is one more reason why the American Dream is slipping out of the reach of so many families. It is perhaps the hardest one for us to solve through government and yet one that we simply cannot ignore. And that is the decline of the family itself.

The American economy isn't the only thing that has changed since my parents came to this country. Since the 1950s, marriage has declined and the number of babies born to single mothers has soared. We can no longer afford to ignore the connection between the health of families and the health of the American Dream.

It's not even controversial: Social scientists, economists, think tanks from the left-leaning Brookings Institution to the right-leaning Heritage Foundation—everyone except too many politicians—agree that the health of the family is key to upward mobility. Brad Wilcox of the University of Virginia studies marriage and its effects on income and well-being. He has found that young people are 44 percent more likely to graduate from college if they are raised by their married parents. Children from intact families are also about 40 percent less likely to have a child outside of marriage.[8]

These are the two things—getting an education and avoiding having children until marriage—that are increasingly key to achieving the American Dream. They are two critical parts of what social scientists call the "success sequence": First get an education, then get a job, and don't have children until you are married. Studies of census data show that if all Americans first finished high school, worked full-time at whatever job their education qualified them for, and then married at the same rate that Americans got married in 1970, the poverty rate would fall by an astonishing 70 percent.[9] Young Americans who follow the success sequence have only a 2 percent chance of falling into poverty and a 75 percent chance of making it to the middle class.[10]

Big government fails now more than ever because it ignores the importance of the success sequence and the family unit. It views the breakdown of families as a product of poverty—not as the cause of poverty. As a result it promotes antipoverty programs to support families instead of pro-family programs to eradicate poverty.

The fact remains that there is no government program—no matter how well intentioned or how generously funded—that has ever or could ever hope to achieve for American families what they can achieve by following the success sequence. It works regardless of whether you're Hispanic, black or white, female or male, college or high school educated. It is, in short, proof of the proposition that in America you can still achieve success no matter who you are. So why isn't the health of the family a bigger part of our conversation on saving the American Dream? Why aren't politicians and Hollywood celebrities and everyone who claims to care about helping people get ahead in America shouting this from the rooftops?

For conservatives, talking about family structure inevitably leads to charges of racism, sexism or somehow trying to force our religious beliefs on others. Political experts ceaselessly lecture us that this is no way to win elections. Liberals seem to think questioning such issues is judgmental and unjust. On issues of family and values, the Democratic Party, the party of big government, becomes curiously libertarian.

This is no coincidence. Proponents are careful never to state it outright, but at the heart of the big-government approach are two central messages. The first is that government is our national family now. The role that husbands, wives and parents have traditionally played in the American family, this approach asserts, can now be safely assumed by government. When it comes to managing your health care, government—not the consumer—knows best. The same logic applies to the schools your children attend, how you save for your retirement and even how you choose the light bulbs for your home.

The second unspoken message of the government-centered approach is the same message that those who believe income inequality is the central challenge of our time believe: that growing the economic pie to benefit the poor and middle class is no longer possible. The only just course is to use government to adjust the size of the slices.

The minimum wage debate is a good example of this. Not surprisingly, raising the federal minimum wage from $7.25 an hour to $10.10, as the president has proposed, polls well—people like the idea of more money. But there's no getting around the law of demand: When you make something—even labor—more expensive, people buy less of it. The Congressional Budget Office predicts that an increase of the minimum wage to $10.10 could cost as many as five hundred thousand jobs.

My family and I saw this firsthand last spring when we stopped for lunch at a Chili's in Broward County, Florida. We were surprised to find what looked like an iPad on the table. The hostess who seated us explained that this mobile device would be our server. On it, we could tap items we wanted to order and pay the bill by swiping our credit card. It reminded me that a machine had just replaced at least one server in Florida. If we raise the minimum wage, companies like Chili's will be driven to replace workers with machines sooner than planned.

In fairness, the same CBO report said that nine hundred thousand Americans would benefit from the wage hike. But who are those Americans? Rather than mothers and fathers struggling to support families, the data show that over 74 percent are childless adults or teenagers. Just 16 percent are married parents with kids.[11] So it's true that an increase in the minimum wage polls quite well, but in practice it would cost half a million American jobs. Some will benefit, but most won't be the hardworking parents who need help the most. If the goal is to help those struggling the most in the current economy, there are better ways to go about it than raising the minimum wage.

What are those ways? In response to calls to raise the minimum wage, conservatives typically double down on policies to grow the economy and create jobs. This approach is correct in the long term, of course. Economic growth is ultimately the answer. But in the meantime, people are hurting, the minimum wage is something people understand and they hear only that conservatives are against it.

Stagnant wages are a real concern to millions of Americans.

We can't just tell people what we are against. We also have to outline what we are for. We can find creative answers that help struggling families while staying true to our small-government principles. For instance, one way to help low-wage workers—both single moms struggling to support kids and single men in need of a foothold in the world of work—is to provide wage subsidies to targeted workers. I have proposed a targeted wage subsidy plan that I discuss in detail in Chapter Three. For now, suffice it to say that it would effectively boost the wages of workers without forcing the cost on employers.

Yes, it is government help for struggling families. But it would not have the job-killing effects of mandating that employers pay employees more than the market will bear. Yes, it involves government spending, but primarily by reallocating money we are already spending. Most important, it is the right thing to do, not just for struggling American families, but for the good of the country as a whole.

The American economy has changed, but our government has not only failed to change with it, it has made the challenges of the new economy worse. Jose and his family are living examples of this. Big government's complicated rules are keeping him from going back into business for himself. Its tax and regulatory policies are crushing innovation and investment. Its commitment to protecting the educational status quo does nothing to help Jose acquire the skills he needs for a better job. And its stale ideas, like increasing the minimum wage, don't help Jose realize the American Dream. They just define the dream down.

Chapter Two

MAKING AMERICA
SAFE FOR UBER

O n Monday mornings I teach a class on political science—
Florida politics, to be exact—at Florida International University in Miami. It makes my mornings at home a little more
hectic, getting the kids out the door to school and getting myself
to campus by eight a.m., but it's worth it. Teaching is rewarding
and it gives me a sense of what young Americans are thinking
these days. More often than not, my students surprise me.

In one class last year I overheard my students talking about
how easy it is for their friends in Washington D.C. to get a ride
home after a night out on the town. They use a service called Uber,
they said. Uber was pretty new to Americans at the time—and
nonexistent in Miami. Like most young people, my students are
excited by the possibilities of technology to make their lives better.
(And when you add partying to the mix, their level of interest
multiplies exponentially.) What they didn't know then was that
Uber wasn't just in Washington but in cities all over America, and

even in Europe. It's an app that you download to your phone, set up an account and enter your credit card information. When you're ready to go home, the app locates the nearest car and sends it to your location. It's quick and easy, and no cash changes hands.

The students in my class were genuinely intrigued by this innovative service and wondered why they didn't have it in Miami. I explained to them that it was because of regulations created by government. Politicians, I said, had passed rules to stifle competition that might threaten their constituents and supporters in the existing taxi and sedan service industry. In Miami, for example, there was a government-created cap on the number of sedan medallions allowed in the city. That regulation effectively shut out any competition to the existing car service companies—competition like Uber.

As my progressive young students listened to me explain why government was preventing them from using their cell phones to get home from the bars on Saturday night, I could see their minds change. They went from fervently believing that big government is necessary to protect the little guy to realizing that big government is often used to stick it to the little guy. Before I knew it, I was talking to a bunch of twenty- and twenty-one-year-old anti-regulatory activists.

It was another one of those times when my students surprised me. The entire identity of liberalism as a political movement is built on the idea that liberals stand for the less powerful, that big government is necessary to fight big business. But as my students learned, the truth is often the opposite. More often than not, big business co-opts big government—and vice versa—and they work together. After all, big corporations can afford to influence government, and the little guys can't. And the more power government has over the economy, the more those with the power to influence government win. Big business uses its influence to create regulations— typically under the guise of public safety or some other seemingly unassailable good—that it can afford to comply with but smaller companies can't. Aided by the indispensable help of the coercive power of the state, big business gains a competitive advantage. Those of us without lobbyists on retainer have less opportunity, higher prices and less choice as a result.

Some call this "crony capitalism." Both parties are guilty of it, but for liberals it presents a serious ideological challenge. After all, if the effect of liberal big-government policies is to put the powerful ahead of the powerless, what exactly do liberal progressives stand for? My Senate colleague and liberal populist hero Elizabeth Warren had a point when she told a MoveOn.org audience last year that "the game right now in America is rigged. It is rigged so that those at the top keep doing better and better, and everyone else is under increasing pressure, is under increasing economic strain. The rules don't get better for America's middle class. The rules are getting better for those who are a thin slice at the top." As I said, Senator Warren had a point—it just wasn't the point she thought she was making. It is *government* that is increasingly rigging the game against the working and middle classes.

A good example is a guy named Brad Soden and his marvelous invention, the Tankchair. Brad has been described as a "robotics savant." But he's really just a regular guy—he didn't even go to college—with a talent for engineering and a wife, Liz, whom he loves. In 1999, Liz was in a car accident that left her paralyzed from the waist down. To make it possible for her to continue to go on family hikes, Brad began designing and building a wheelchair that could go off-road. He worked mostly in his garage at first, using whatever he had on hand—a lawn mower engine, an old air-conditioning unit. By borrowing some ideas from the army's Bradley Fighting Vehicle and remote-controlled fighting robots, Brad eventually came up with the Tankchair. One writer described the Tankchair as "a wheelchair in the same sense that an aircraft carrier is a boat."[1] Instead of wheels, it has tracks. It can climb hillsides, traverse beaches and go up to thirty miles per hour.

Brad Soden's gift of independent movement to his wife has since become Tankchair LLC, a family company that employs Brad, Liz and Brad's parents. They custom build about two hundred chairs a year. Brad is a veteran and a lot of his customers are wounded warriors. He'd like to expand his business and employ disabled vets to build more chairs. What's standing in his way is crony capitalism. Government is by far the single largest purchaser of power wheelchairs, through Medicare. If a company can't get Medicare reimbursement for its power wheelchairs, that company can't be competitive. But getting certified in order to be reimbursed by Medicare can cost a manufacturer up to $1 million in meeting government safety and other regulations. This government-created barrier to entry into the power wheelchair market has allowed the big manufacturers who can afford to get into the market to hugely inflate their costs without fear of being undercut by competition. One report found that Medicare pays these manufacturers four times what it costs to make power wheelchairs. The bill for this overpayment, of course, is ultimately paid by all of us. Meanwhile, Brad Soden, an innovator, entrepreneur and humanitarian—everything we should be encouraging in our economy—is frozen out of the market.

———

We're all familiar with government picking winners and losers in the "green" energy market—mostly losers, it turns out, like the failed solar panel manufacturer Solyndra. The rampant crony capitalism in the green energy field is only the beginning of the story, however. As I will discuss in Chapter Five, the Affordable Care Act contains a provision that has been called a "slush fund" to guarantee that participating insurance companies don't lose their shirts from Obamacare. When I introduced legislation to remove this bailout provision from the law, I was flooded with calls from insurance company executives telling me they couldn't participate in Obamacare without the provision. These were the same executives, by the way, who had lobbied to get the law passed. The "slush fund" was their reward for supporting the law. With it, they won't lose money even if premium prices go through the roof. Instead, the taxpayers will pay the bill.

Crony capitalism takes what we need most for our economy today—innovation, investment and a level playing field for competition—and squelches it. When big government and big business get together, political conformity—not innovation—is rewarded. Government spending crowds out private investment and companies that aren't favored by government can't attract private investors anyway. Most blatantly of all, this competition is the opposite of fair. To "unrig the game," as Senator Warren might put it, we need less investment in government and more investment in America. We need to reward innovation, not political access. Most of all, we need a level playing field for U.S. businesses, large and small.

Ending crony capitalism is made more difficult by the fact that these programs are always passed in the name of helping the middle class and struggling Americans. To sign the ineffectual, pork-filled 2009 stimulus bill, President Obama traveled all the way to Denver instead of walking to the Rose Garden. Why? His press secretary explained that the trip "shines a light on the issues that average Americans are facing." It makes me think of an "average" American family I've become acquainted with, the Broyleses, and how they fared under another law that was passed to "help" them.

Daniel and Becky own a small home furnishings store in Orlando called Foreign Accents. They sell unique handcrafted items from all over the world. The recession hit their business hard. Walk-in traffic to their store vanished. Longtime clients dropped them, and their biggest contracts were terminated. To survive, they turned to putting expenses on multiple credit cards. They knew it was a desperate move, but they had no choice. Sure enough, it backfired. After a few missed payments, the banks hiked their interest rates and the debt on their shoulders began to compound.

At this point—as in every time of trial in their lives—Daniel and Becky turned to their faith to get them through it. With three boys who depended on them, they prayed every day that God would reveal the right way forward. Becky considered going back to school in order to get an outside job, just so they could have a steady income stream and hopefully some benefits. But despite all the talk and all the spending in Washington, jobs remained scarce—good jobs were practically nonexistent. Taking a flier on finding decent outside work didn't seem like a safe bet against the cost of going back to school.

Eventually, around 2012, the Broyleses' business began to turn around. A couple contracts for hotel banquet tables started trickling in. Customers started returning to the shop again. Business wasn't what it had been before the recession, but it was enough to break even and keep the debt from rising. And then, just when Daniel and Becky had convinced themselves to continue working hard to keep the doors of their business open, the government stepped in to "help" them again. The Affordable Care Act hit the Broyles family—and thus their family business—hard. Their health insurance premium had been rising by small amounts each year for a while. But when the law went into effect in 2013, it shot up from $520 to $660. Worse, their deductible doubled, from $2,500 to $5,000. They couldn't afford it, so they dropped their coverage and turned to a faith-based program called Medi-Share, which allows members to spread out the burden of health care costs and coverage.

Daniel and Becky's business is still operating—for now, anyway. They love their work and they draw great meaning from it. Their oldest son helps out while he works toward his online bachelor's degree. They're not bitter, but you sense that they feel the system is stacked against them. Any success they have seems to come despite the mandates coming from Washington.

The Broyleses' story is a graphic, real-life example of how our political leadership—from both parties—is failing families who can't afford to influence the agenda in Washington. What they really need is not another expansion of the federal government disguised as help for the middle class. What they need is a strong and growing free-enterprise economy. This has been Washington's greatest failure of all. It has failed to put in place policies that would foster such an economy in this new century.

Fostering a strong and growing free-enterprise economy in the twenty-first century means meeting four fundamental challenges: making America the best place in the world to invest and create jobs, keeping America the global leader in innovation, ensuring access to markets and consumers for American products, and winning the global competition for the most talented and innovative people. It's fair to ask how meeting these challenges would help a struggling home furnishings store in Orlando. The answer is the same way it helped my father when he was tending bar in Miami or the way it helps the hardworking Uber driver in Washington D.C.: through the wealth-generating multiplier effect of an unfettered market economy. American investment and ingenuity creates jobs and careers in building automobiles and airplanes, creating personal computers and the Internet, or discovering new biomedicines and developing apps for smartphones. Then the people who have these jobs buy houses. And when they need to decorate their houses, they come and see Daniel and Becky Broyles.

Our first challenge is to make America once again the best place in the world to invest and create jobs.

There was once a time when there were only a handful of countries you could possibly invest in with any degree of confidence. But now there are dozens of developed economies capable of and willing to host new investment. This is good news for global prosperity. But for America, it also means we have competition. Today, capital investment moves freely across borders, landing wherever it can generate the best return. Americans are in a daily contest to attract investment here, to persuade investors to start a new business or grow an existing business in our country instead of abroad. In this contest for global investment, the United States has put itself at a great disadvantage.

As hard as it may be to believe, the country that produced Ford Motor Company, IBM, Microsoft and Amazon has the highest corporate tax rate of any advanced economy in the world. Combining federal and state taxes, our corporate rate is nearly 40 percent. The global average is under 25 percent. On the basis of taxes alone—putting aside the cost of regulations and labor—it is more expensive to invest and create jobs in America than in most other developed economies in the world. If we stick with this status quo, we risk losing the next great American company before it has the chance to begin. Already every day seems to bring news that yet another company has relocated its headquarters to Canada or Ireland. Liberals question the patriotism of companies that do this to avoid high U.S. taxes, but they fail to acknowledge that this behavior, although regrettable, is perfectly rational, even necessary to survive in a global economy in which we have stacked the deck against our own companies.

This is especially true when it comes to smaller and midsize employers. After all, politically connected corporations are able to carve out loopholes in the tax code that shield them from its anti-competitive effects. General Electric is the poster child for this. While GE may not have reduced its tax burden to zero as was reported in 2012, it's safe to say it didn't pay the full 40 percent.

But what happens to the employer that can't hire a large law firm to find the loopholes? What happens to the employer that can't hire the Washington lobbyist to create the loophole? What happens is that either they open overseas or, more likely, they never open at all.

It starts with not having access to the money to open up in the first place. Over 70 percent of new businesses are launched using savings or by borrowing against assets, particularly houses.[2] But the housing crisis all but choked off this source of investment funds. Therefore, making it easier for people to start new business in America begins by giving people access to more of their own money. Utah Senator Mike Lee and I have dedicated ourselves to begin to accomplish this through the development of a new, modernized tax reform plan. Our plan is broad and fundamentally both pro-growth and pro-family. I will discuss the pro-family aspects of the plan in Chapter Five. As for the plan's pro-growth emphasis, it rests on creating new investment in American jobs by lowering taxes and leveling the playing field.

Because so many small and new businesses pay their taxes on personal income tax returns, our proposal integrates both the individual and business sides of the tax code in order to put small businesses on an even footing with big corporations. It prioritizes replacing our current business tax system with a new, globally competitive model. Instead of carving out exemptions for favored industries that have lobbyists, we propose a pro-growth tax code that treats all employers equally, regardless of their business structure. Furthermore, our plan would allow American employers to be more competitive with foreign companies by lowering our tax rate on businesses.

We also propose allowing employers to immediately deduct every dollar they invest back into their business. The Treasury Department estimates this deduction would stimulate investment about four times as much as lowering the tax rate. The reason is simple. Being able to immediately expense investment would apply only to new investment, incentivizing businesses to undertake more of it.

As it stands today, when a business calculates its taxable income each year, it is allowed to deduct only its operating expenses, like wages, materials and taxes. Investment expenses, like new buildings and machines, are treated differently. Businesses generally aren't allowed to immediately deduct these expenses. Instead, they have to pay taxes on that money and then write the costs off over several years or even decades. The result is that the current system discourages employers from reinvesting their profits back into the business to grow it, because deductions years in the future are worth less than deductions today. Our plan would change that by allowing all companies to take a full and immediate tax deduction on all the income they reinvest in their business.

Take the example of a business that brings in $50,000 per month, with $20,000 in basic operating costs. The owner has to decide whether to withdraw and spend the other $30,000 or to use it for investments that would grow the business, allowing it to hire more people. Under the current system, the safe thing to do is to withdraw and spend the money.

But under our plan, the company will immediately deduct every dollar that it reinvests back into the business. By allowing immediate expensing of investments, this cash is more likely to be invested, boosting productivity and leading to increased wages and the hiring of new workers. The more a business invests, the less the federal government will get to take away.

Our current tax system also encourages companies to keep the money they make abroad, and in many cases to incorporate abroad instead of in the United States. About 15 to 20 percent of the products made in the world are made by American companies operating overseas. We would like to see these companies bring the money they have made abroad back to America. We want them to invest their profits earned abroad to create new jobs here.

But our current code has the opposite effect. Under our current tax laws, if they bring this money back to America, they pay U.S. tax (with credit for any taxes paid abroad). As a result, there is an estimated $2 trillion of American corporate profits sitting in bank accounts overseas. To put it in perspective, this is equivalent to the total annual size of the German economy.

The answer is what is called a territorial tax system, under which companies are not taxed on profits brought home from abroad. The fact that the vast majority of developed economies in the world already have a territorial tax system—including all other G8 nations—has put American companies at a major competitive disadvantage. By keeping American firms competitive in the global marketplace, a territorial tax system will lead to job creation and reverse the recent trends of stagnant wage growth.

The second challenge posed by the new economy is to preserve and strengthen America's position as the global leader in innovation.

In their fascinating book *The Second Machine Age*, MIT's Erik Brynjolfsson and Andrew McAfee envision a future in which America can turn the challenges of the new economy into opportunities for better and more prosperous lives. Brynjolfsson and McAfee argue that we are at a historical technological turning point. Improvements in digital hardware, software and networks are combining to create an economic and lifestyle shift every bit as sweeping and profound as the industrial revolution.

The possibilities are genuinely exciting. Innovations that were previously confined to episodes of *Star Trek* are being realized in rapid succession. Brynjolfsson and McAfee predict we will have autonomous—self-driving—vehicles in our lifetimes, creating millions of hours of productivity for harried soccer moms and commuters. And not only have we created a computer that can beat a human at *Jeopardy!*, that computer is now going to medical school and its diagnostic capabilities are being uploaded to the cloud for the benefit of all humanity.

These exciting predictions come with a big caveat, however: This second industrial revolution and the bigger economic "pie" it will create won't necessarily benefit everyone, unless we change the way we prepare Americans for the workforce. Brynjolfsson and McAfee correctly argue that we need to transform our education system to meet the employment needs of this new, innovation-driven economy. Progress will also depend on government getting out of the way and allowing entrepreneurs to keep inventing new ways to combine technology and human labor to create new industries and jobs.

Today innovation is being stifled by an anti-innovation tax code and by patent trolls who target innovators with actions that are nothing short of legalized extortion. Perhaps most of all, as we've discussed, innovation is being held back by a regulatory code that has become a tool for established status quo industries to shut down new and innovative competitors.

When a group representing the nation's largest financial firms asked businesspeople why America isn't producing as many start-ups as it did a decade ago, the businessmen and -women's second most frequently cited reason (after a lack of qualified workers, which I address in Chapter Four) was government regulation.

The regulations explosion is a bipartisan creation. Both parties and most presidents have done their share to balloon the federal register from 71,224 pages in 1975 to 174,545 pages in 2012.[3] But the current administration has taken federal rule making to new heights. Between 2009 and 2011, the federal government cranked out 106 new regulations, each with an expected cost of at least $100 million a year.[4] In 2010 alone, more such "major rules" were enacted than in any year since at least 1997. One study put the costs of regulation during the first five years of the Obama administration at an astounding $500 billion, more than the entire economic output of Sweden or Ireland.[5]

Regulations cost us in economic growth and job creation because they are expensive to comply with. It is especially costly for small and new businesses that cannot afford the costs of hiring lawyers to help them comply with complicated regulations. These regulations, and the new ones that keep showing up, also create uncertainty. Potential employers are afraid to grow and even start, because they can't predict what the rules will be or how much business is going to cost. And so this uncertainty keeps would-be entrepreneurs on the sidelines and existing businesses from expanding.

For this reason and more, Obamacare has been the single largest impediment to job creation in the United States for the past several years. It is the perfect storm of ever changing federal mandates, costly regulations and aggressive marketplace intrusions. It is difficult to imagine a law more perfectly designed to stifle job creation.

Not all regulations are bad, of course. Some are necessary. We want to know that the water we're drinking is clean and the car we're riding in is safe. But when regulations become too onerous, they function as a hidden tax, making everything we buy more expensive.

Think I'm exaggerating? The Small Business Administration calculated that the total cost of federal regulation in 2010 was $1.75 trillion. Compare that with the $1.09 trillion the government collected in individual and corporate income taxes that year. In other words, the hidden tax of regulation is about 61 percent higher than the taxes that are out in the open.[6]

One of the best ways I know to ease this burden on the American people—not to mention cut down on the crony capitalist habit of using regulations to stifle competition—is to establish a National Regulatory Budget. This would be an absolute dollar limit on what federal regulations could cost the economy in any given year. My plan would create an independent board that would be tasked with estimating the cost of all existing federal regulations. Congress would then be directed to set a ceiling on the amount each agency's regulations would be allowed to cost the economy. If a proposed regulation took the agency over its budget, it would have to find savings elsewhere by repealing old regulations. This would force federal agencies to enact only those regulations that serve an essential role. Under my plan there would be no more blank checks for regulators and the lawmakers who enable them.

One of the most promising examples of the power of American innovation is the energy revolution going on in our country today. The United States is now the fastest-growing producer of hydrocarbon energy in the world. We have been the world's largest producer of natural gas since 2010, and in 2014, thanks to the shale oil boom, we surpassed Saudi Arabia and Russia to become the world's number one oil producer.[7]

This revolution is the product of innovations in energy extraction pioneered in America like fracking. It's important to note that these innovations, which have resulted in a tripling of our oil and natural gas production in a very short time, are due to both American technological know-how and free-market capitalism. Edward L. Morse, global head of commodities research at Citigroup, recently explained: "In only a few other countries (such as Australia, Canada and the United Kingdom) is there a tradition of an energy sector featuring many independent entrepreneurial companies, as opposed to a few major companies or national champions. And in still fewer countries are there capital markets able and willing to support financially risky exploration and production."[8]

The American energy revolution is potentially good news for both consumers and job seekers, but only if we build the infrastructure necessary to catch up with the innovations in extraction that we've pioneered. Production is up, but our construction of pipelines to move that energy to market hasn't kept up with the pace, largely due to government-created obstacles.

The Keystone Pipeline debacle is just the beginning. Well-paying construction and trucking jobs are being held up because of an ideological agenda that says energy extraction is always bad, despite the tremendous efforts that have been made to protect the environment. Unlike other necessary infrastructure projects, building pipelines doesn't involve any taxpayer funding. The private sector stands ready to create these jobs, but government is saying no by throwing up bureaucratic hurdles to the construction of new pipelines. Our regulatory review process produces lots of litigation and red tape, but little else. A case in point: A private company is interested in building a natural gas pipeline into Florida. But before it can even begin construction, it is being forced to spend months under the review of six different federal agencies.

We can do better than this and still protect our environment. We should explore ways to streamline the regulatory review process for natural gas pipelines. And we must eliminate the barriers that prevent us from exporting natural gas and oil abroad, such as the outdated ban on crude oil exports that dates back to the 1970s.

Beyond the production of hydrocarbons, it's also critical that we remain a global pioneer in energy research. Here I will break with some of my more conservative friends and concede that the federal government has a limited but important role in supporting basic research. The Department of Energy operates a system of national labs—think Los Alamos National Laboratory in New Mexico or the Oak Ridge National Laboratory in Tennessee— that have long been a leading source of basic research into things like alternative energy and the human genome. But they currently lack the ability to work with the private sector to translate this research into commercial products and services that will produce American jobs.

One of the problems has been that the government insists on attempting to dictate which research projects have commercial potential. But if there's one thing we learned from the Obama administration's failed taxpayer subsidies of companies like Solyndra, it's that the government is a lousy venture capitalist. The cutting-edge research being done at the national labs is too valuable to be left to the bureaucrats. Some research has commercial applications; some doesn't. The job of determining which is which is better left to the market. I have joined with Democratic Senator Chris Coons of Delaware to propose legislation that will make it easier for our labs to work together with private businesses to bring groundbreaking research to fruition in the marketplace. It's one more way we can defy the naysayers and maintain America's inno-

vative edge—and the jobs that go with it—in the twenty-first
century.

═══

Beyond taxes and regulations, another challenge to American investment and innovation is our lack of progress in ensuring access
to markets and consumers.

In the digital age, this competition for access begins on the
Internet. Whether it's selling jeans on Amazon, showcasing your
products on Facebook or creating a start-up with Kickstarter, the
Web has transformed the way we do business. And this revolution
will not slow down. As much of our lives as we already spend online today, Web traffic is expected to be thirteen times higher by
2017.

The Internet is a political success story as well as an economic
one. The Web has not only helped democratic movements across
the globe to organize, it has given the world a window on the actions of dictators and tyrants to suppress freedom. Ensuring free
and open access to the Internet is not just an economic necessity.
It is central to human freedom. Not surprisingly, that openness
and access is threatened today. Forty-two countries restrict their
own people's access to the Internet. Many of these countries now
want to take their repression global by taking control of how the
Internet is governed.

But the reason the Web is a singular success story in the history
of human organization is that it has avoided such government control. It is currently overseen by a diverse group of independent boards,
user groups, businesses, nonprofit organizations and others—in

other words, it hasn't been controlled so much as managed. Free from government interference, the Internet has been hailed as the greatest "deregulatory" success of all time.

But this sort of freedom is the exception rather than the norm. The story of mankind is sadly one where powerful nations try to force their way of life on weaker nations and peoples, or control the means of commerce and trade, primarily land, the seas and the skies. Even today, for totalitarian governments like Russia and China, Internet freedom is increasingly intolerable. These nations say they would like to see the Internet subject to international control, by which they mean the United Nations. But no committee of bureaucrats sitting in Turtle Bay could attempt to control a global network of trillions of Web pages without doing cataclysmic damage. And no international organization that allows Cuba on its "Human Rights Council" should be given the opportunity to try.

That is why opposing this sort of takeover and preserving Internet freedom must be a top national priority. Internet freedom isn't just about being able to surf your favorite Web pages; it is about being able to sell your products and services to people all over the world online. In this new century, the harder it is to do that, the harder it will be to grow our economy and create jobs.

In 2012, I sponsored bipartisan legislation supporting an Internet free of government control. It passed both the Senate and the House without a dissenting vote. This was a good start, but ongoing threats to Internet freedom—including the uncertainty surrounding the Obama administration's announcement that the United States is relinquishing its role in administering Internet domain names—require more action. The United States must declare unambiguously that the current multi-stakeholder, decentralized model of Internet governance is the official policy of our country. Not only that, but we must prevent the transfer of the administration of domain names to a foreign government or governmental agency.

The corollary to preserving the freedom to innovate using the Internet is, of course, being able to exercise that freedom. And here, wireless spectrum—the radio waves that allow commerce, as well as cat videos, to be transmitted on the Internet—is essential. With a growing amount of Web traffic now being conducted on wireless devices, spectrum is among our most valuable national resources today.

But it is also a finite resource. Wireless spectrum is the interstate highway system of the digital world. It is the road we use to "commute" online, and the highway is getting mighty crowded and increasingly subject to traffic jams. As more people come online, the traffic is only going to get worse.

Thankfully, there is a solution. Today the federal government "owns" what some estimate is almost two thirds of the most valuable and sought-after wireless spectrum. In typical fashion, government being government, the agencies involved are reluctant to share just how much spectrum they have or whether they are using it efficiently. Whatever the exact numbers are, it is unacceptable that sixty federal agencies control more spectrum than is available to a nation in which the number of mobile phone subscriptions is higher than the number of people.

To fix this, I have introduced legislation that reallocates spectrum used by the federal government to be used by commercial wireless services. The taxpayers will win because the spectrum auctions will raise money for the Treasury. The government will win because it will have its spectrum needs protected and met more efficiently. And the American people will win when our most precious natural resource is put to better use to grow our economy. The resulting innovation will create thousands of jobs.

Outside of cyberspace, creating new markets for American products is done the old-fashioned way, through carefully crafted trade deals with other nations. The emergence of a global middle class has created more potential customers than ever for our products and services, yet our trade barriers and domestic restrictions keep too many American businesses out of these emerging international markets.

First and foremost, we need trade policies that make it easier for our products to reach a global network of consumers. When I talk to Americans about expanding trade, I often hear from people who believe that free trade is a destroyer of American jobs. After years of opening up our markets to trade and investment from others but not getting reciprocal access from countries like China, for example, I understand people's wariness about deals that shortchange American companies.

Trade deals that are truly two-way streets, however—deals in which access to markets is fair and reciprocal—can be net job creators for Americans. Take the example of my cell phone. Embossed on the back of it are the words "Designed by Apple in

California. Assembled in China." But when all these phones assembled in China are sent here, they have to be off-loaded in American ports. Those are American jobs. Then they have to be transported to distribution centers—more American jobs. Then they have to be transported to stores, where they're sold—more jobs—at a lower price. Those savings are now available to be spent elsewhere, helping to create still more jobs.

Forgive the Econ 101 lecture, but it's an important point. Carefully crafted trade policies could be a boon to tens of thousands of American small businesses, not to mention consumers. That is why I support trade promotional authority for the president. And it's why I support continued efforts to pursue regional and bilateral trade agreements—such as the Trans-Pacific Partnership with developed economies in Asia and Latin America, and the Transatlantic Trade and Investment Partnership with Europe.

The need for trade to find new markets for American products reminds us why foreign policy is still important, even at a time when we are rightly focused on the struggles of the middle class here at home. The United States has to be engaged in the world in order to sell its goods and services to the world. We can't afford to lose markets because a country is afraid of what its more powerful neighbor will do if they trade with us.

This is exactly what happened in Ukraine. They sought closer economic and political relations with the West, and Russian strongman Vladimir Putin made them pay a price for it—and was allowed to do so by the United States and other free-market powers. In the twenty-first century we have to be able to sell our products and services to any market in the world. By failing to force

Putin to pay a price for his naked aggression in Ukraine, we have set an example for other countries with hegemonic aspirations. We are telling not just Russia but China, Iran, North Korea and other countries that it's okay to intimidate their neighbors if they seek trade and economic relations with us. They now look at Ukraine and they see a cautionary tale that directly affects our economy: If we grow closer to the United States and the West, this is what will happen to us.

Last but certainly not least, winning the global competition for investment and innovation will require us to win the global competition for talent. We simply cannot remain competitive in the twenty-first century if we are unable to attract and keep the most talented people in the world.

For as long as there has been an America, we have benefited from the infusion of entrepreneurs, innovators, workers and dreamers who have come to this country from other lands. But today, at a time when so many working-class and middle-class families are struggling, it can fairly be asked: Is it possible to advocate continued immigration while at the same time fighting for an agenda to lift up the working and middle classes? Aren't these two things at odds with each other? Well, the answer is yes—if we continue on the path we're on.

To begin with, our immigration system itself is chaotic. Entire sectors of our southern border are not secure, creating not just an immigration problem but a serious humanitarian and national security one as well. Last summer's crisis of thousands of unaccompanied minors entering this country proves that both our borders and our immigration system can be overwhelmed very quickly. In addition, many of our immigration laws are simply not enforced or unenforceable. For example, a significant percentage of those here illegally arrived legally, but then overstayed visas. We do not know who most of them are or where they are.

Our immigration system, designed primarily to reunite families, is an outdated relic of the last century. This system worked for much of the twentieth century, when we had no shortage of low-skill, middle-income jobs and the government safety net was still fairly limited. But today we have low to nonexistent growth, a shortage of good jobs and a massive web of needs-based programs.

No nation on earth is more generous when it comes to immigration than America. Each year about one million people permanently immigrate here legally. But when people hear that we have over twelve million people here illegally, they feel as if we are being taken advantage of. They see how hard it is to find and keep a steady and well-paying job, and they worry that more people will mean more competition for already scarce work. That's not nativism. That's human nature.

It does not have to be this way. We *can* have an America in which a thriving middle class coexists with continued, orderly, legal immigration.

We must begin by reigniting economic growth and opportunity in this nation. When our economy is growing and thriving, employment isn't a zero-sum game. A new American's gain does not have to be an existing American's loss. If that were true, every time we hand out a high school or college diploma to one person we should hand an unemployment check to someone else. In fact, the opposite is true.

That's why, just as in all the other conservative reforms discussed in this book, having an immigration system that works for our country begins with economic growth. Indeed, instead of being an impediment to equal opportunity and widely shared prosperity, the right immigration system is a critical component of economic growth. One study by former Congressional Budget Office Director Douglas Holtz-Eakin found that if we modernized our immigration system from a family-based one to one focused on merit and productivity, we could grow the economy by almost a full percentage point in the near term and raise per capita growth by over $1,500.

Our current system is damaging our economy. Each year our colleges and universities graduate foreign students who are among the best and the brightest in the whole world. Instead of putting them to work here, innovating products and creating jobs, we send them back to China and India to compete against us. This makes no sense. If one of our college graduates is a world-class basketball player, there is little doubt he will wind up staying to play in the NBA. But if he or she is a world-class scientist, we make them leave!

Making our legal immigration system a merit-based system that encourages innovators will have broad benefits for our economy. Studies show, for example, that 40 percent of American Fortune 500 firms were started by immigrants. What's more, roughly half of the most successful start-ups in Silicon Valley were started by people who weren't born in this country. And since 2000—despite the restrictions we have on merit-based immigration—over a third of the American Nobel Prize winners in chemistry, medicine and physics have been immigrants. This kind of scientific and entrepreneurial activity generates jobs across the income spectrum—from corner-suite executives to construction workers and IT engineers. Just the kind of jobs that help Americans rise to the middle class and beyond.

Transitioning to a merit-based, high-skilled immigration system would also help immigrants assimilate more quickly and easily into American economic and civil life. As reform conservative authors Yuval Levin and Reihan Salam have written, a merit-based system—in conjunction with formal civic education requirements, such as a test on American history and government before being granted a green card—would have the effect of allowing immigrants to integrate more successfully into American communities and reduce the isolation and poverty of many of today's immigrant communities.

The benefits of a merit-based legal immigration system are widely (although not universally) accepted in America. So why, then, has nothing been done about it? The reason is our illegal immigration problem. We will never have the votes needed in Congress to modernize any part of our immigration system until the issue of illegal immigration is adequately dealt with first.

A significant percentage of Americans simply don't trust either party in Washington to address other aspects of immigration reform before illegal immigration has been brought under control, and for good reason. The immigration reform law of 1986 legalized more than three million people who were here illegally, but the enforcement measures were never fully implemented. For years

President Obama, his allies in Congress and many immigration reform supporters have told us that the border was "as secure as ever." This fallacy was dramatically exposed when portions of our southern border were essentially overrun in the early part of 2014. Then there are the numerous examples of President Obama simply ignoring, suspending, rewriting and violating the law through executive action. All of these things have left many to conclude that, no matter what enforcement mechanisms are written into law, this administration will simply ignore them. The result is a stalemate on an issue of critical importance.

So what is the way forward? First, we must make the argument that reform is needed at all. I have heard some argue that all we need to do is enforce the laws we have already. But that is not accurate. On the enforcement side, we need additional investment in electronic monitoring and personnel. Building more fencing alone will not be enough to address illegal crossings. We also need to give employers a reliable way to check the legal status of the people they hire. We need to invest in an entry and exit tracking system to prevent visa overstays. All of this would require reform.

How do we achieve this reform, given the current stalemate? We must begin by acknowledging that, considering our recent experience with massive pieces of legislation, achieving comprehensive reform of anything in a single bill is simply not realistic. Having tried that approach, I know this to be true firsthand. The fear that such massive pieces of legislation include some clever loophole or unintended consequence makes it even harder to achieve. The only way we are going to be able to break this impasse and make progress on this issue is in a sequential and piecemeal way, with a series of bills that build upon one another until ultimately we have put in place the kind of immigration system our nation needs.

The first step must be enforcement measures that are effective and verifiable. Such measures would include securing the most vulnerable and most trafficked sectors of the southern border, mandatory E-Verify and the full implementation of an entry-exit tracking system.

The second step is to modernize our legal immigration system toward a merit-based one. That would mean reassigning existing visas away from family-based immigration and toward work- and skill-based immigration, passing reforms for high-tech visas, as well as creating a limited guest worker program for seasonal workers in the agricultural sector to reduce the incentive for these workers to come here illegally in the future.

Once both of these reforms have been passed, then I believe the conditions will be in place to address the most politically sensitive aspect of immigration reform: what to do with more than twelve million people currently here illegally.

On the one hand, calls to grant amnesty to twelve million people are unrealistic and quite frankly irresponsible. On the other hand, not a single opponent of the Senate bill I helped author proposed that we try to round up and deport twelve million human beings. So how do we deal with this dilemma? I believe that if the enforcement measures are in place, there exists a path forward that would obtain a significant majority in Congress and the support of a majority of Americans across the political spectrum. It consists of three parts.

First, those here illegally must come forward and be registered. If they have committed serious crimes or have not been here long enough, they will have to leave. With the new E-Verify system in place, they are going to find it difficult to find a job in any case.

Second, those who qualify would be allowed to apply for a temporary nonimmigrant visa. To obtain it they will have to pay an application fee and a fine, undergo a background check and learn English. Once they receive this work permit, they would be allowed to work legally and travel. To keep it, they will have to pay taxes. They would not qualify for government programs like Obamacare, welfare or food stamps. And if they commit a crime while in this status, they would lose their permit.

Third and finally, those who qualify for a nonimmigrant visa will have to remain in this status for at least a decade. After that, they would be allowed to apply for permanent residency if they so choose. Many who qualify for this status will choose to remain in it indefinitely. But those who choose to seek permanent residency would have to do it the way anyone else would, not through any special pathway.

This three-step plan is not only the best way to reform our immigration system, it is, in my opinion, the only approach that has any chance of success. An overwhelming majority of Americans in both parties would support this sort of incremental approach. Of course, there will be detractors. Some will continue to call for less immigration and more deportations. On the left, some will continue to demand an all-at-once-or-nothing-at-all approach.

Just like saving Medicare and Social Security, immigration reform is a powerful political issue. Some on the right know it needs to be done, but they want someone else to do it. Some on the left have concluded that having the issue is more politically valuable than solving the problem. Groups on both sides use it to raise money.

In the end, immigration reform is fundamentally about reforming government and restoring the American people's faith in the ability of their government to do basic things right. I don't believe this challenge will be fully met until we have new leaders in Washington who support both the rule of law and the job-creating potential of the free market. Until then, the best way to rebuild trust and reform our broken immigration system is through incremental steps both to fix our immigration system and to realize the full potential of our country.

Why? Because the American Dream is not small. It's not about entitlement. It's about opportunity. It is not about parceling out prosperity to the few. It is about a striving, growing prosperity for anyone willing to work hard and to dream. Conservatives have always been the keeper of this flame. We have always been the believers in a growing, striving America. It is a tragedy that today we find ourselves being portrayed as pessimists about America's potential rather than the optimists we have always been. We will miss a great opportunity to reclaim the true meaning of our movement—and, much more important, to restore the true potential of our country—if we fail to act.

All of these reforms are important in their own right, but each is like a single brushstroke. Only when they are combined together do we see what they create: a picture of a growing, striving, thriving America in the twenty-first century.

Imagine the opportunities that will open up for the American people when economic growth creates jobs, lifts wages and restores hope. Imagine the country we can create: A private sector liberated from excessive regulation. Start-ups free to compete on a level playing field with established businesses. An economy reinvigorated by technological innovation and trillions of dollars of new investment. New markets for American products and ideas. Secured Internet freedom and abundant wireless spectrum to boost innovation. The American economy will take off at a historic rate, creating hundreds of thousands of high-paying jobs.

This is the exciting opportunity before us. This is the unavoidable challenge that awaits. We no longer have the luxury of wasting time on the failed promises of big government or the divisive rhetoric of class warfare. The world around us is changing quickly, and we have waited for far too long to change with it.

Chapter Three

EQUAL OPPORTUNITY, EQUAL DIGNITY, EQUAL WORK

The war on poverty turned fifty last year in the midst of a changed debate over income and justice in America. When President Lyndon Johnson launched the war in 1964, the issue was the plight of the poor. For many of Johnson's ideological descendants today, the issue is very different. Income inequality—the growing gap between the very rich and the rest of us—is sucking up lots of political oxygen these days. The subtext of this debate—and very often the text—is how the rich can be brought down to somehow make our society more equal. What's lost is any discussion of the question that animated President Johnson: How can the poor be lifted up to make our society more prosperous for all?

Down in Plant City, Florida, Christine Miller is focused on other, more practical questions—like making people use her parking spaces. She runs an emergency food bank that served almost twenty-three thousand people last year. Most of her "clients," as she calls them, are genuinely needy and genuinely appreciative.

But there are some who are of a more entitled mind-set. They like to drive up in front of the warehouse and demand their food. So Christine and her staff have had to institute a "park first" policy. It's a small part of their attempt to do more for their clients than just hand out food—and that begins with showing respect for her and her staff.

Christine has been at the Tampa-area food bank for three years, so she has seen a lot. She grows quiet when she talks about a man and his adult daughter who came in when she first started working there. As soon as she saw them, Christine knew something was very wrong. The woman looked dazed and there was stress—and real fear—in the man's face. When his daughter went out to the car to retrieve her purse, it all came spilling out. Just days before, the daughter's husband had shot himself in front of his wife and children. Desperate and in shock, the woman had brought her kids to live with her father. Now they needed help just to put food on the table. So Christine did what she could: She gave them a box with enough food to feed the family for the next four or five days.

The experience haunts Christine because she knew the family needed more—in that case, grief counseling, at a minimum. Most people who come to the food bank need more. Some of their needs are simpler than others. Many don't know that they can ask their bank for forgiveness if they bounce a check, for instance, or that there are alternatives to the exorbitant fees charged by check cashing businesses. One of Christine's first projects at the food bank was to bring in a financial literacy program called Money Smart. For people at or below the poverty level, the program teaches financial basics like maintaining a checking account, the importance of saving and how to repair and/or preserve your credit. The program has made a difference, Christine says, especially for those she struggles most with how to help: the people who genuinely want to lift themselves and their families. One woman who went to her first Money Smart class—a grandmother who had to take in her three teenage grandchildren when their parents were both incarcerated—is now a regular volunteer at the food bank. It is a small victory, but one Christine will take.

Officially, the United Food Bank of Plant City exists to provide emergency rations to people who have signed up for food stamps but aren't yet receiving them. But Christine and her staff always make sure their clients are also signed up for all the other government assistance they are eligible for. In this way, the Plant City food bank exists as a bridge between destitution and the vast bureaucracy of federal programs for the poor.

The war on poverty has resulted in a tangled web of at least ninety-two often overlapping, often duplicative federal programs, including seventeen separate food aid programs, twenty different housing programs and twenty-four programs dedicated to job training.[1] In fifty-one years of metaphorical war, some $15 trillion has been spent on these programs, $799 billion in 2012 alone.[2]

Despite all this, Christine and her staff see only deepening need in eastern Hillsborough County. Their clients are single moms and grandmothers, the newly out of prison and a lot of returning veterans. More and more, she says, the people walking in her doors are the formerly middle class. She and her staff have had to learn that just because someone pulls up in a nice car or lists an address in one of the nicer neighborhoods around Plant City, it doesn't mean they're not in trouble. It can take two years for the bank to foreclose on a home, and in the meantime the occupants could be flat broke. And selling their car isn't an option—chances are it's their lifeline to job interviews and plain old survival. Not to mention that replacing it with trashed credit is next to impossible.

Some former donors have even showed up, now as clients. "When you see them and you hear their stories—'My husband is out of work, I just found out my daughter's pregnant and I don't know what to do . . .'" Christine's voice trails off. "They don't even know where to go for help because they've never needed it before."

Christine is on the front lines of what President Johnson called not just a war but an "unconditional war" on poverty. When he made that declaration, 17.3 percent of Americans were poor. Today, the rate is almost unchanged at 15 percent. When you factor in higher costs for things like health care and transportation, the number of men, women and children living in poverty comes to forty-nine million—that's one in six of all Americans.[3]

Some argue that the war on poverty has been "won," citing as proof the vast government bureaucracy that has been built to wage it. This assistance has helped many people, and that is no small thing. But our efforts remain incomplete because it has also created a system in which millions of Americans live cushioned but not buoyed by government assistance. Government has succeeded in trapping far too many into poverty as a way of life, and it has not done nearly enough to help Americans escape poverty. A tragic 70 percent of children born into poverty today will never make it to the middle class.[4] The uncomfortable truth is that there are now a number of other countries with as much or more opportunity than ours for the poor and middle class. More people in Canada, for instance, go on to surpass the income of their parents than in the United States.[5] Fifty-one years later, there is no other word for this than failure.

Christine finds meaning in her work—"I'm definitely right where God wants me," she says. Still, she sees a void that she struggles to fill every day. Her job is to hand out food, but her clients need so much more. She'd like to help them escape their circumstances, not just survive them. She isn't given to lofty expressions of patriotism, but her concern for her clients comes from the same place that motivates those of us worried about the American Dream. The difficult truth is that America is still the land of opportunity for most, but it is not the land of opportunity for all. If we are to remain an exceptional nation, we need leaders dedicated to finding creative new ways to lift up the poor. Sadly, what we're getting today is the opposite: a lot of talk about stale old policies to bring down the rich.

The reasons so many Americans are stuck in the kind of poverty that Christine Miller sees every day are varied and complex. The modern economy has eliminated many low-skill jobs and the jobs that are left require the kind of education our schools aren't delivering to the poor. Most significant of all, too many American children are born into communities where marriage is a vanishing institution. I will have much more to say about this in Chapter Seven, but for now I'll just note this: It is no coincidence that 71 percent of poor families with children lack a married couple to provide for them.

The root causes of poverty are deep in family and education, but the immediate cause today is pretty straightforward: not enough jobs and not enough Americans working. In 2012, only about 11 percent of the poor were working full-time. Most of the poor in their prime working years—from eighteen to sixty-four— hadn't had even a single week with a job.[6] And just as it is true globally that free enterprise, not foreign aid, eliminates poverty, so is it true here at home. According to Keith Hall of George Mason University, there has never been a decline in the poverty rate that wasn't associated with a rise in employment. As a matter of fact, in the past twenty years work seems to be the only thing that can be relied on to reduce poverty.[7]

But the disappearance of work in America isn't just confined to the poor. The number of able-bodied adults who are working today has fallen to a thirty-six-year low. Less than 63 percent are in the labor force. This is the equivalent of between seven million and eight million people giving up on finding a job. Part of the reason for the decline in work is expected—the retirement of the baby boomers. Part of it is still not completely understood—the changes in the economy due to technology and globalization, which we've discussed. But for the poorest American families, the decline of work has had particularly disastrous consequences. Families with little or no savings, no assets in a home and no partner in marriage to share the load are the families that can least afford to not work.

Not only are the roots of poverty complex, but poverty affects different parts of the country differently. We're used to thinking of the poor in America as being concentrated in big cities, but the fact is poverty is more widespread in rural areas than in cities. The Census Bureau has identified 353 persistently poor counties in the United States and 301 of them—over 85 percent—are rural counties.[8]

The recession has made poverty in America even more diverse. It hit children in rural areas harder than children in the cities, so much so that children living in deep poverty—in families surviving on less than $1,000 a month—are now more numerous in rural areas. The recession also increased poverty in the suburbs. Between 2000 and 2010, the growth in the number of people living below the poverty line was twice as high in the suburbs as in the cities. Today there are actually more poor people in the suburbs than in the cities.[9]

Add to this the fact that there are regional, racial and ethnic differences in poverty as well. The poorest Americans are concentrated in the rural areas of the Southwest, the northern Midwest, the Southeast and on Native American lands.[10] In the Southwest many are Hispanic, in the South many are African American and in the Appalachian Southeast many of the poor are white.

Not surprisingly, the poor struggle with different challenges in different parts of the country. Transportation is a major issue for the rural poor—the nearest grocery store or hospital may be thirty or forty miles away. Cars aren't luxuries there; they're necessities—necessities that too often break down and always require gas. Similarly, in the suburbs there may be public transportation to and from the city, but not to the local supermarket or doctor's office.

And in the cities housing costs eat up more of a family's budget than elsewhere—often because of government zoning regulations.

Poverty in America is as diverse as America, and yet Washington has a one-size-fits-all approach to fighting it. Instead of finding new and innovative ways to address unique needs, the federal government has piled on duplicative agencies and programs to address the same need. Oren Cass, an adviser to Mitt Romney in 2012 who has written about giving states more flexibility to fight poverty, describes a web of programs created through different pieces of legislation and administered by different agencies with different rules, procedures and eligibility requirements. What freedom states have to administer programs is complicated by the many strings attached by the federal agencies that fund them.

We shouldn't be surprised. For fifty years our antipoverty policy has been guided by the idea that more and better-funded Washington programs administered by bureaucrats who know better will help the poor. As time has passed, these programs have acquired constituencies in the special interests that benefit from them. As programs grow, the forces encouraging their continued growth multiply and the process perpetuates itself. Anyone who questions the status quo—questions, that is, not whether we have an obligation to help the poor, but merely whether the current course is the best way to do so—is declared to be an enemy of the poor.

Taken together, all of this makes it highly unlikely Washington will be any more successful in the next fifty years in lifting Americans out of poverty unless we pursue real and fundamental change. We need a dramatic shift away from the mentality that says one more federal program, one more bureaucracy or one more pile of money will successfully lift the poor. We need to move away from the tired old debate about inputs—how much money we spend—to an honest examination of outputs—how many American lives we can change.

When Lyndon Johnson announced the war on poverty, he gave away his big-government vision by saying, "The richest nation on earth can afford to win it." I see America—and our obligation to ensure opportunity for the least fortunate among us—differently. I believe that the most *creative and innovative* nation on earth is uniquely qualified to lift the poor by putting Americans on a path to prosperity and self-sufficiency. To unleash that creativity and innovation, I have proposed the most fundamental change to how America fights poverty and encourages income mobility since President Johnson conceived of the war on poverty fifty-one years ago. At its center is the best antipoverty measure we know of: work.

———

As she struggles to do something more to help her clients, Christine Miller knows the importance work has in improving their lives. To that end, Christine has formed relationships with a hair salon and a dry cleaner. Now if a client is going in for a job interview, she and her staff can set them up with a new haircut and some decent clothes.

"That's where I'm hoping to give them a hand up as opposed to just a handout," she says.

I have yet to talk to anyone who works day in and day out with

Americans struggling with poverty and a lack of mobility who doesn't know what Christine knows. They all seem to emphasize some combination of the same three themes:

- the importance of the person in poverty taking responsibility for herself and her future
- the importance of addressing the whole person, not just the immediate need
- the importance of work

The top-down, Washington-controlled war on poverty has failed all three of these tests. Federal poverty programs are good at alleviating immediate needs by providing food and health care and writing checks. What they have failed to do—in truth, what they have rarely even tried to do—is to encourage and to help people to take that first step toward responsibility for themselves and their families by working.

Conservatives like to talk about incentives, and for good reason—incentives matter. One big reason we have failed to move more poor Americans to work and self-sufficiency is that we haven't given them the right incentives to do so. Here I'm not talking about the negative incentives sometimes favored by conservatives that tell the poor to pull themselves up by their bootstraps or suffer the consequences. I'm talking about offering the poor positive incentives to move from welfare to work—giving them a reason to become independent, not just a reason to avoid being poor.

As they exist, our antipoverty programs discourage moving from dependency to work by effectively levying a large tax on anyone who earns too much to receive benefits. House Budget Committee Chairman Paul Ryan calls this the "poverty trap." For understandable reasons, most poverty programs offer decreased benefits as poor people make more money. This functions like an extremely high tax on the poor, particularly those in low-wage jobs, which is most of the poor. If people work and make more money, they lose more in benefits than they would earn in salary. At a time when jobs are scarce and wages are stagnant, the poverty trap is catching more Americans than ever. Programs like the Affordable Care Act double down on this work disincentive.

The poverty trap isn't just a bug in our antipoverty programs—it's a feature. To change this, we need nothing less than a transformation of our approach to fighting poverty. A well-intentioned desire to help the poor has succeeded in making government dependency more remunerative than work. A similarly well-intentioned desire to help the poor must now make work pay again. This can be accomplished through two significant but achievable changes in policy. First, give the states real freedom to create innovative programs to encourage work among the poor. Second, improve the current federal wage subsidy to keep them working.

In this transformed approach to fighting poverty, these two changes work together. States find creative ways to do what Christine is trying to do: provide relief for the nonworking poor that incentivizes and capacitates work. Then the federal government makes the transition to work profitable and sustainable. The goal, always, is independence and self-sufficiency through work.

The idea is to take the hundreds of billions of dollars' worth of federal antipoverty funds and consolidate them into something I call a "Flex Fund." The Flex Fund would be just what it sounds like: a fund that distributes a lump sum payment to the states to use to support or create innovative and multifaceted state and local antipoverty programs. This change recognizes that there is no silver bullet to ending poverty, that it will take many different approaches for many different areas where poverty is found.

The animating principle behind the Flex Fund is this: Government has an important role to play in helping the poor, but it should be the government that's closest to the people it's trying to help. I first became convinced that the fight against poverty should be a local one when I was in the Florida legislature. Miami-Dade County, where I live, is a pretty representative microcosm of poverty in America. We have inner-city poverty and rural poverty as well as the working poor. Most of the poverty issues I dealt with as a legislator and then as speaker of the house had to do with children. Many of these are kids born into broken families, living in substandard housing in poor neighborhoods or in rural isolation. They're zoned out of good schools. Maybe they're being raised by their grandmother. And this has been going on for generations. I realized that the odds of these kids making it out of poverty are almost zero unless something dramatic happens in their lives.

It was about that time that I heard about the Harlem Children's Zone. I was so intrigued I visited the project in 2007 and saw something that could never have been conceived of by bureaucrats in Washington, much less implemented effectively. Geoffrey Canada and his teams go into neighborhoods and literally envelop poor children from before birth to college graduation with the education and support they need to rise out of poverty. The idea is holistic change—to break the cycle of poverty not just for the child but for the whole neighborhood.

I like the idea so much I sponsored a bill in the Florida legislature that established the Miami Children's Initiative, which is taking the same holistic approach to Miami's Liberty City, another area of concentrated multigenerational poverty. When Cecilia Gutierrez-Abety and the good folks at the Miami Children's Initiative started to run into trouble with all the strings attached to federal funds, it occurred to me that there is a better way.

The Flex Fund would allow states to support projects like the Miami Children's Initiative by allowing them to both fund and administer their program without federal interference. Under the Flex Fund and Wage Enhancement Credit, total antipoverty funding would be unchanged, but states would be required to spend the Flex Fund allocations on antipoverty programs that are consistent with the purposes of the federal programs they are replacing. The amount of money each state would get would be determined by the number of people in poverty in that state. An individual state's funding would increase if its population in poverty increases. But, critically, if poverty goes down, the state would be allowed to keep the extra money, no strings attached. With this "shared savings" funding formula, states would be incentivized to find ways to actually eliminate poverty, not just cut spending on poverty programs.

I know from my time working in state government that states are capable of coming up with creative and innovative new ideas if given the flexibility. Utah is an example. While Washington replays the same debate over how and whether to extend traditional unemployment insurance, Utah is experimenting with ways to get people into well-paying jobs. In a pilot project, Utah required people who had been out of a job for six months or more to take online training courses in order to continue receiving unemployment benefits. The courses focused on skills needed for modern professionals, with topics spanning from résumé building to career direction to interview skills.

The state tracked the progress of the participants and found that their professional preparedness to go back to work improved so much that what had begun as a requirement quickly turned into a sought-after tool. Thirty-six percent of participants found the courses so helpful that they voluntarily completed more training than required. Most important, the online training helped them find a job faster. Among the test group, unemployment duration was reduced by 7 percent.

The program has now gone statewide in Utah, and a 7 percent reduction in duration of benefits is expected to save $16 million dollars annually, not to mention the boost to the state's economy and culture from a more engaged labor force.[11] Not surprisingly, other states are taking notice. A similar program was attempted in Mississippi with even better results. Participants there increased their preparedness by a staggering 31 percent.[12] And in Kentucky, workers spent 2.2 weeks less on unemployment insurance benefits when required to take training courses.[13]

The beauty of the Flex Fund is that it will make states accountable for how they spend their federal antipoverty funds in ways they aren't today. It's the difference between spending someone else's money and spending your own. When it's your own, you care more about results. As it is, the funding formula for programs like food stamps and Medicaid contains a perverse incentive for states: It rewards them with more federal dollars the more they spend.

Some states are pretty good at gaming this arrangement. In one case, states were taking advantage of a provision in federal poverty regulations that made families who were receiving benefits through a federal home heating assistance program eligible for additional food stamps. To boost their food stamp funding, states were signing up residents for a single dollar of home heating assistance. They called it "Heat and Eat." When Congress tried to tamp it down by requiring that families receive at least $20 in home heating assistance to get more food stamps, the states responded by spending more of their home heating funds—most of which came from the federal government anyway—in order to preserve higher food stamp funding. Democratic New York Governor Andrew Cuomo proudly announced that he would spend $6 million in federal home heating funds in order to get $457 million in food stamp funding.[14] This example is telling. As long as the current incentives to spend someone else's money exist in our poverty programs, some states are going to take advantage of it. Giving states their own funds to spend and be accountable for through the Flex Fund would put an end to this kind of abuse of the American people's taxes and their goodwill.

After serving eight and a half years in state government, I know that if free to innovate and if responsible for their own spending, the states could implement programs that give those currently stuck in low-wage jobs access to a job training system. They could offer relocation vouchers that would help the long-term unemployed to move to areas with more jobs. They could remove the marriage penalties in safety net programs like Medicaid. They could enact a nearly infinite number of other nimble and targeted reforms to address the needs of people in their communities whom they know and understand in ways Washington D.C. never could. Their funding would remain about what it currently is, but if history is any guide, costs would decrease as new state initiatives move people from dependency to self-sufficiency. Ultimately, my proposal isn't intended to increase or decrease the amount of federal funding spent on antipoverty programs. My approach is intended to take us from tired old battles about money in Washington D.C. to new ways to cure poverty at its root.

In my proposal, revitalized state poverty programs under the Flex Fund will work hand in hand with a new federal wage enhancement tax credit to encourage and reward work. The philosophy behind the federal Wage Enhancement Credit is summed up very nicely by Robert Doar, who was in charge of implementing welfare reform for New York City between 2007 and 2013. One of the things he learned, Doar says, is "making work pay is welfare reform too."

He should know. Doar and his colleagues were spectacularly successful in moving New Yorkers from dependence to independence. The city's welfare rolls were reduced from more than a million recipients to fewer than 350,000 between the passage of welfare reform in 1996 and Doar's departure in 2013. More important, work rates increased, dependency decreased and child poverty fell. Today, even in the aftermath of the recession, child poverty in New York is almost 10 percentage points lower than it was before welfare reform.[15]

How did they do it? Doar gives the lion's share of the credit to the work requirements in welfare reform. Under the law, welfare recipients had to be working or looking for work in order to receive benefits. According to Doar, when it came to getting off welfare, nothing substituted for a job—not education, not training. New Yorkers who were quickly employed stayed employed longer. Work participation rates rose faster than even the most enthusiastic welfare reform advocates had anticipated—even among never married single moms.

It takes a vibrant private economy to create jobs, but the New York example highlights how government can play a role in getting people in these jobs and keeping them there. The most successful government antipoverty programs are the ones that don't try to substitute for employment but instead help people get employed and stay employed. The clunky-sounding Earned Income Tax Credit (EITC) is one such program.

The EITC works by providing a tax credit for low-income families that work—but only to families that work. It effectively boosts wages by dramatically lowering taxes on low-wage workers. And because it's a refundable credit, families can get a check even if they make too little to owe income taxes. It has been shown not just to encourage work, but to decrease poverty as well. The Census Bureau found that the poverty rate in 2011 would have been a full 3 percentage points higher—up to 19 percent—if it weren't for the EITC and the Child Tax Credit.[16]

The EITC embodies the right philosophy: the importance of work, even for low wages, as the gateway to self-sufficiency. But it has significant shortcomings. It is paid only once a year in a family's tax return, making it hard to plan a monthly budget around. And it's a complex credit. That means the IRS makes lots of mistakes in awarding it and most families that claim it use professional tax preparers, which eat up a lot of their refund.

There's a better way for government to support work. I have proposed that we build on the success of the EITC by substituting it with the Wage Enhancement Credit for low-income workers. Under my plan, workers making less than $20,000 would receive a monthly 30 percent credit from the government. This would allow an unemployed individual to take a job that pays, say, $18,000 a year—which on its own is not enough to make ends meet—but then receive a wage enhancement to make the job a better alternative to collecting unemployment insurance. This wage enhancement would gradually diminish up to a yearly income of $40,000.

Unlike the EITC, which delivers the wage subsidy in a once yearly lump sum, the Wage Enhancement Credit would be delivered monthly through a check from the Treasury. So instead of blowing the money on year-end vacations or flat-screen TVs, the money is more likely to be used for monthly living expenditures or even saved. Moreover, the wage enhancement would function like an increased minimum wage but with a critical difference: It would increase available jobs rather than decrease them. Nor would it force employers to pass higher labor costs along to consumers.

An important final difference between the Wage Enhancement Credit and the EITC is that my proposal is directed at the individual, regardless of family size. It makes little sense not to encourage noncustodial fathers to work and be able to support their children. And as I will discuss in Chapter Seven, the marriage crisis that is at the heart of poverty and low mobility in America today is in many ways a crisis of marriageable young men. Unlike raising the minimum wage, which will reduce the available jobs for young fathers, supporting their wages and encouraging their work will help reintroduce the institution of marriage to a population that desperately needs it. And in order to ensure that families with children aren't adversely affected by my proposal, part of my opportunity agenda includes an expanded Child Tax Credit. I will discuss this tax credit as well as my plan for a family-friendly tax code in Chapter Five.

Together, the Flex Fund and a federal Wage Enhancement Credit would transform our approach to poverty by turning the dead end of government dependency into a pathway to work and independence. Because the system gives states new accountability for their antipoverty programs—and rewards them if they are successful—states will create incentives for the poor to prefer working and receiving the Wage Enhancement Credit to not working and collecting assistance. In fact, the states would be smart to use their Flex Funds to pay for greater wage enhancements for workers to further incentivize work. And once the poor have taken that first step through working, they're more likely to stay on the path to self-sufficiency.

⸺⸺

It has been eye-opening to me how many roads to restoring the American Dream lead to education. The ultimate opportunity equalizer—the ultimate wage enhancer—is a good and relevant education. But the children of the poor begin the race for the American Dream three steps behind the rest. It's no wonder, then, that so many are failing to catch up.

The education necessary for good jobs doesn't end once you're in the workforce. For those in low-wage jobs especially, training in the skills necessary for the jobs of the new economy is essential. But many don't have the time or the money to pursue a traditional higher education. We can help them by bolstering and reinvigorating our nation's existing job training system, giving high school students the skills that lead directly to well-paying work after graduation.

As usual, local communities are racing ahead and waiting for the federal government to catch up. For instance, in Miami, one local school district has partnered with a car dealership to create an innovative approach to career education. The Braman Automotive Training Center is a free vocational training program for inner-city high school students. Students spend six months in the classroom and then a year getting on-the-job training in Braman's service, parts and body departments. Each student is paid for his or her work and is paired with a senior employee as a mentor. There have been two graduating classes so far, and with the help of the program all graduates have found jobs, either at Braman's or at other automotive shops. This is just one example of how we need to change our education and job training approach. While our workforce delivery system must be driven by states, the federal government can help address the shortage in many skilled-labor jobs by creating more pathways toward obtaining these certification credentials and by encouraging alternatives to the traditionally accredited.

The millions of people currently trapped in poverty and low-wage jobs are a tremendous untapped resource. Just think of what it would mean for America to gain full use of the talents and abilities of all its people. They would develop new innovations to improve our lives, or help build the next great American company. They would be doctors in our hospitals and scientists in our labs. They would be customers for our businesses and partners in our investments. They would be leaders in our government and pastors in our churches. Imagine how much greater a country we would be if the dreams and talents of over forty million human beings were unleashed into our economy.

As with many Americans, this fight is personal to me. My mother was one of seven girls whose parents often went to bed hungry so their children wouldn't. My father lost his mother when he was nine. He left school and went to work at about the same age of my youngest son now.

I'm one of the blessed ones, and I try to never forget it. I live each day one generation removed from poverty, grateful to my grandparents, to my parents and to my country. Our status as a land of equal opportunity has made us a rich and powerful nation, but it has also made us a special one. It has transformed lives and families. It has given people like me the chance to grow up knowing that no dream was too big and no goal out of reach, that the son of a bartender and a maid could have the same dreams and the same opportunities as the son of a millionaire or a president.

Now there are millions of Americans trying to access these same opportunities. There are struggling parents trying to give their children the chances my parents gave me. There are children growing up like I did, with dreams just like mine. Whether or not they get the chance to improve their lives will determine whether we remain a special place, or become just another country.

For when America ceases to value opportunity, work and independence for all, we will cease to be America. What makes our country special is that we don't just fight poverty—we honor work. Work, and the sense of purpose and accomplishment that it brings, is essential to human happiness. Arthur Brooks of the American Enterprise Institute calls this "earned success." That means achieving success—whether you define that as making money, raising good kids or mentoring seventh graders—on your own terms through your own hard work and merit. Brooks cites studies that show that people get less happiness from unearned things—even good things like money—than they do from things they've earned through work. For Christians, the centrality of work to human meaning and happiness comes from our being made in the image of God. Being made in His image means we have dignity, worth and creativity. Work is how we use these gifts to contribute to our fellow men and women and to honor His name.

Fifty years ago we set out on a big-government approach to fighting poverty and for fifty years we've been doubling down on that approach, tinkering around the edges at best. It has failed and this failure not only morally implicates all of us, it goes to the heart of the health of the American Dream. Now is the time to try a new approach.

Chapter Four

MAKING COLLEGE A GOOD INVESTMENT AGAIN

As dreams go, Kristi's isn't what you'd call outrageous. She wants a job and a life, in that order. But at age twenty-nine, Kristi has become cynical about the American Dream.

"You're told that life is supposed to be a certain way," she says. "You go to high school, then you go to college, then you graduate and get a job. Then you get a husband and a white picket fence and a dog and a cat and a son and a daughter and life is just grand."

This isn't how life is working out for Kristi. She had the great misfortune of graduating in late 2006 from the University of Central Florida (UCF), at a time when the Florida economy was the leading indicator of the Great Recession to come. But long before the grass stopped being cut in the yards of foreclosed homes across Florida, the job market that Kristi would face when she graduated had begun to change. The industrial manufacturing economy that had created once great cities like Detroit and lifted millions into the great American middle class was long gone. What was left in its wake was a postindustrial economy in which jobs that could be outsourced to cheaper labor and less regulation overseas had been, and jobs that could be automated were rapidly being taken over by machines and technology. By the time Kristi took her last exam at UCF, it wasn't just that jobs were harder to find; it was that the jobs themselves had changed, and the higher education system she had just left hadn't kept up with the change.

Kristi grew up in Apopka, Florida, outside Orlando, where her parents own and operate a greenhouse construction company. She had a pretty comfortable middle-class life. That she would go to college was never really in question—and for good reason. The value of a higher education has never been higher than it is for her and other members of the millennial generation, meaning those born after 1980. The unemployment rate for graduates with a bachelor's degree or more in 2014 was 3.8 percent, compared with 12.2 percent for those with a high school degree.[1] Although it's no guarantee you won't get laid off, a college degree means having a better chance of keeping your job, even in today's economy. When the federal government tracked the high school class of 2004, it found that 40 percent of those with high school degrees and 45 percent of high school dropouts had lost a job within the past six years, compared with just 19 percent of those who'd gotten their bachelor's degree.[2] In addition, college graduates earn more—an average of $17,500 more per year—than high school graduates. In 1965, when my parents were supporting a family with less than high school educations, that gap was only $7,500.[3]

The reason the gap between high school and college graduate earnings has grown is more evidence—as if we needed it—of how much our economy has changed. College graduates are outpacing high school grads not because their earnings have grown that much, but because the earnings of high school graduates have *shrunk* that much. When my parents first came to this country, the typical high school graduate earned 81 percent of the salary of a college graduate. Today's high school graduates earn just 62 percent of the salary of those with college degrees. But it's not just the difference between driving a new Audi and driving a used Toyota that's at stake. Today, not going to college increases your chance of living in real poverty, the kind of deprivation in which a family of four survives on around $23,000 a year. In 1979, just 7 percent of high school graduates were this poor. Today that number is a depressing 22 percent.[4]

No matter who you are or who your parents are—black, white, Hispanic, rich or poor, educated or less educated—getting a college degree significantly raises your chances of success in America. The poorest children increase their chances of escaping poverty from 55 to 84 percent if they get a four-year degree. Not only that, their chance of making it all the way to the top to be among the wealthiest Americans quadruples with a college degree.[5] This effect stands in direct refutation of those who argue that the American Dream is dead for the poor and minorities.

These data about the mobility that comes with a higher education are compelling, but they beg a significant fact: First you have to get one. It's like the old Steve Martin joke about the secret to becoming a millionaire. It begins, "First, get a million dollars . . ." A college education may be the surest route to making it in America today, but for millions of Americans, being prepared for that education and being able to afford it are the real road-blocks to the American Dream. And here, who your parents are and how much they make does, unfortunately, make a difference. Higher-income high school graduates are more likely to go to college—and more likely to stay in college—than the less well-off. They can better afford to, for one thing. Plus, they usually have another advantage that we're only just beginning to truly appreciate: They are more likely to come from intact, two-parent families and communities that encourage achievement, responsibility and self-restraint.

A college degree is still a good investment, but for middle-class families the math on affording one is terrifying—and getting worse. Even as the typical family's income has declined 6.6 percent since 2000, the cost of going to a private college has increased 24 percent—and that's after adjusting for inflation. For public universities, allegedly the less expensive route, the increase was 37 percent.[6] This relentless climb in tuition rates, moreover, seems impervious to what's going on in the economy as a whole. Even when the Great Recession took hold five years ago and Americans had less to spend, tuition kept rising, even accelerating in its rise. Between 2006 and 2012, the cost of college increased by 16.5 percent.[7] By the 2013–2014 school year, students and their parents could expect to pay an average of $40,917 a year to attend a private four-year college, and $18,391 to go to a public one.[8] For would-be collegians and their parents, these prices are devastating. For parents of young children, they're virtually prohibitive. The parents of a baby born today may never have to worry about her driving her own car or learning to write cursive, but they will need to save

$150,000 to send her to a state school, and almost double that if she wants to go to a private college.

The competing pressures of the importance of a college degree and the high cost of getting one are putting Kristi and millions of Americans like her in a bind: They can't afford to go to college, and they also can't afford *not to go* to college. The cost of a higher education is rising at a time when it's worth more in future earning power than ever before. The only way out of this conundrum for students like Kristi is to go into debt. For others of less means, there is no way out; the challenge of affording to go to school—and to stay in school—is too great. Students from the poorest American families are now graduating from college at the lowest level in thirty years. Fewer than 10 percent get their degree.[9] Overall, only 58 percent of full-time students who entered college in 2004 graduated within six years.[10] For the rest—those who attend some college but fail to graduate—the burden of student debt is truly tragic. They face the worst of all possible outcomes: having taken on debt without obtaining the credential to allow them to make enough to repay it.

The resulting situation confronting American families is a curious one—one that says a lot about the dysfunction of our higher education system. Despite the demonstrated positive wage effects of a college degree, 57 percent of American adults now believe our higher education system fails to provide good value for the money it costs.[11] At a time when Americans should value a college degree most, they increasingly doubt its worth. Colleges and universities are pricing out what should be eager customers. How is it that some enterprising entrepreneur hasn't come up with creative ways to educate Americans for the modern workforce that don't involve harnessing students with unsustainable debt?

Kristi is a good example. While she was at UCF she landed an internship with one of the largest McDonald's franchisers in central Florida. She was responsible for the "point of purchase" advertising in the restaurants. That meant that if Barbie was featured in the Happy Meals that month, she had to make sure that there was Barbie advertising in the store and at the drive-through window to entice customers to make a last-minute impulse purchase. She loved the job and she was good at it. It inspired in her a love of marketing that she pursued all the way through a degree in interpersonal communications at UCF.

Getting the degree took her four years. She had to quit her part-time job in order to take the classes required to graduate because they were offered only at certain times. Because she couldn't work, she had to take on $9,000 in debt. Did Kristi necessarily need her college to certify that she was credentialed in marketing? Why did she need to go into debt for a degree when most of what she really needed to learn she could learn on the job? What about an apprenticeship option while she attended classes? And why weren't there more online options for the required classes so she could keep her job?

Why? Because our higher education system is resistant to creative, innovative change, that's why. It's a heavily regulated cartel that uses government to protect itself from outside competition. Students like Kristi, understandably drawn to the higher earning potential promised by a college education, are paying more and more and getting less and less. We now have a twenty-first-century economy with a twentieth-century higher education system. The jobs of today demand skills that colleges and universities are failing to deliver and students are failing to demand. Something has to give.

For college students and their families, the new economy presents challenges, but also opportunities. It creates new jobs that actually pay more than the ones they are replacing. To fill these jobs and exploit these opportunities, however, the new economy requires new skills and new ways of educating workers. Americans need help bridging this skills gap. This is a central challenge of restoring our economic mobility—and one that we are failing today. More than anywhere else, the journey to restore the American Dream begins around the kitchen tables of America, where families like Kristi's are struggling with whether a college education is an investment they can afford to make.

Spend any time in Washington and you become familiar with something called the law of unintended consequences. It's pretty much what it sounds like: Even well-intended government policies can have unfortunate consequences. For decades, America has laudably endeavored to expand access to higher education by expanding Americans' access to student grants and loans. This policy has made it possible for more of us to go to college—that's the intended consequence. The unintended consequence is that the ready availability of federal student loans has led to an explosion of student debt. Because they can, and because they have to, more and more students are taking on debt—70 percent of bachelor's degree graduates have debt when they leave school, up from less than 50 percent of the class of 1994.[12]

While overall consumer debt grew by 43 percent between 2003 and 2013, student loan debt ballooned by more than 300 percent. In just one year, 2013–2014, student debt grew 10 percent while overall debt grew just 1.6 percent.[13] The sad result is that the class of 2014 was the most indebted of all time, with the average borrower owing $33,000 on graduation day. That's almost double what student borrowers owed twenty years ago, even after adjusting for inflation, with the result that a record one in ten students with loans have defaulted on their debt—the highest level in a decade. But last year's grads shouldn't feel too bad. They inherited the Most Indebted title from the class of 2013, and will likely pass it on to this year's graduating class.[14]

Increasing access to federal student loans has been a bipartisan effort in Washington, one that I have supported. But it has created what many experts believe is a bubble in higher education, not unlike the housing bubble that preceded the financial crisis. College investment costs are rising faster than returns. The open spigot of federal student loans flowing into colleges and universities has become a cost-free government subsidy. Colleges and universities can raise tuition higher and higher in the knowledge that the government will continue lending students as much as they need. Students continue to easily borrow their way into unsustainable debt without demanding more from higher education institutions.

The result has been to turn students into bad consumers and colleges into unaccountable sellers. Because no one has called them on it until now, higher education institutions have been free to use this torrent of federal loans to do lots of things that don't have much to do with preparing their students for the modern economy. One study found that the number of administrative employees at colleges and universities (think deputy assistants to the associate vice provost and gender equity administrators) has more than doubled over the last twenty-five years, outpacing the growth in students by more than two to one.[15] Some schools, desperate to attract students at their increasingly exorbitant prices, have poured federal dollars into high-end amenities like luxury dorms and state-of-the-art athletic facilities. Wine bars are popping up in student unions. Some schools are offering the ultimate undergraduate enticement: the single dorm room with its own bathroom.[16]

It's a statistic you've probably heard: American students collectively owe over $1 trillion in debt—$1.25 trillion to be exact, according to the Federal Reserve.[17] Of course, student loan debt isn't experienced collectively, as a number on a ledger or in a political speech. It's an individual burden that is altering—and in many cases limiting—the lives of millions of young Americans. To begin with, student debt isn't like other kinds of debt. It can't be expunged through bankruptcy, and it has a nasty habit of lingering in the lives of its owners. Kristi knows this firsthand.

For a while after graduation, things went well for Kristi. She had a job she liked—with the McDonald's franchise, no less—for about a year and a half. Then, in December 2008, she got laid off. Still in debt and out of work, she started cutting back expenses where she could. She moved back in with her parents. But she soon discovered the trap that awaits the unemployed with student debt.

"You can defer maybe one car payment a year," she says. "But you can't defer a credit card payment. You can't get out of the contract with your cell phone. You can't defer car insurance. The only bill you can defer is student loans."

So Kristi deferred. She got another job in January 2009, but when the company went under that September, she deferred again. After a long stretch without a job, the car dealership she worked for in college hired her in September 2012—and then laid her off early in 2014. She deferred payment on her loans once again. Today, Kristi is eight years out of college and unemployed. And because her student loans continued to accrue interest even when she was deferring payment on them, her student debt is actually greater than the day she graduated.

"I owe ten thousand dollars and I graduated eight years ago," she says. "The way it looks, I don't know if it's going to get better or worse. I may end up paying them for the rest of my life. Who knows?"

It's that sense of pessimism—the sinking belief that they will never claw their way out of debt—that is limiting the lives of so many young Americans today. Economists are starting to worry that these young lives put on hold by student debt are dragging down the economy as a whole. In testimony before Congress last year, Federal Reserve Chairwoman Janet Yellen conceded that out-of-control student debt might be holding back the housing market and slowing the economic recovery. A study of the relationship of student debt to business and job creation found that Americans with student loans are less likely to start businesses of their own. Either they can't qualify for a loan given their existing debt or they're afraid to go deeper in the hole.[18]

Student debt is harming the economy by literally preventing young Americans like Kristi from starting their lives. Having a student loan used to correlate with higher rates of home ownership and car ownership. It makes sense. More education used to mean more income, which meant being able to afford things like mortgages and car loans. Not anymore. Young Americans burdened with student debt had lower rates of car and home ownership than those without debt in 2012.[19] More of them live with their parents and fewer are getting a place of their own. The number of households in America rose by 1.35 million a year between 2001 and 2006. In the last seven years, that number is down by more than half, to 569,000.[20] And because consumer purchases like houses and cars are not only the building blocks of individual lives but are also the primary drivers of the economy, we have arrived at a paradox: Investing in our future through higher education is destroying our future, one young life at a time.

How did we get to this point? Expanding access to higher education can't mean driving more and more young Americans into their parents' basements. Solving the student loan crisis doesn't mean we should cut off federal loans to students, nor does it mean we should allow millions of Americans to default. It means building a higher education system that is in sync with the demands of the new economy. It will require new levels of accountability and transparency on the part of both students and universities, turning students into smarter buyers and colleges and universities into more accountable sellers.

I'm one of those Americans who wouldn't be a college graduate if it weren't for federal grants and loans. I understand the temptation to resolve the conflict between the high promise and the high cost of higher education by taking out loans and hoping—praying—they're a good investment. Still, when you're young, essentially clueless and focused on your dreams, it's hard to know for sure.

Evan is a young college grad who still isn't sure. He and I share a love of sports and, with my younger self at least, a certain lack of vigilance about going into exorbitant debt. Evan grew up in Fort Myers, and when it came time to go to college, he knew he wanted to study sports management. He chose Liberty University in Lynchburg, Virginia, over cheaper options closer to home because it is a Christian school where he, in his words, knew he "wouldn't get off track." Liberty also offered a sports management degree. So every semester Evan signed a promissory note for the student loans he needed to pay for his degree. He admits that when he graduated, he had no idea how much he owed.

That is, until he got the letter. A couple of months after graduating in December 2013, Evan got what he calls a "very depressing letter" notifying him that his bill had come due. "It didn't hit me until I got that letter in the mail. It was my lender saying, 'Hey, we're going to start pulling money from your bank account in three months,'" he recalls. He owes almost $20,000. Even though he was working two jobs, his finances were already teetering on the brink. This pushed them over.

I know Evan's pain. By cobbling together the proceeds from Pell Grants, student loans, work-study and summer jobs, I managed to pay for my undergraduate degree without going too far into debt. Law school, however, was another matter. Like Evan, every semester I would sign promissory notes to borrow more money. When I finally got the depressing letter informing me that I was over $100,000 in debt, I had no idea what I was in for.

I've never regretted the money and the time it took to get my degrees, but I do wish I had been better informed about what I was getting myself into. I never sat down and calculated how much I could expect to earn when I graduated or whether it would be enough to cover my loan payments. Even if I had had the foresight to do so, there wasn't a source to tell me how much someone with a law degree from the University of Miami could expect to make. As with Evan, there was no guide to tell me whether the debt I was accumulating was a good investment in my future or a financial anchor that would weigh me down for decades.

The dirty little secret of student debt is that it *is* an investment—and not all investments in college degrees are equal. Some bad investments in college and graduate degrees are—or should be—foreseeable. Joe Therrien, the Occupy Wall Street protestor who left his job as a teacher and borrowed $35,000 to get his master's degree in puppetry, comes to mind. He was last seen, out of work, protesting his plight with his colleagues in New York's Zuccotti Park.[21] Good for Joe for pursuing his passion, but few prospective students can afford to allow only their passion to guide them when it comes to student loans. After our homes, this is the second largest investment most of us will ever make. It's wrong and misguided that conscientious young people like Evan are going into massive debt with little or no information about what the expected return will be.

The fact is, it's no longer enough just to get a degree. If students want to increase their chances of getting a job and decrease their chances of ruining their credit, they have to get the *right* degree. In a report aptly titled "Not All College Degrees Are Created Equal," researchers at Georgetown University found that unemployment rates are highest among recent college graduates in the arts (11.1 percent), humanities and liberal arts (9.4 percent), social sciences (8.9 percent) and law and public policy (8.1 percent). Tellingly, the report found that majors that are more targeted to specific industries have the fewest numbers of unemployed graduates. Health care and education majors, for instance, were more likely to find jobs. As for future earnings, college students and their families should keep their eyes open here. Engineering, computer and mathematics majors get the biggest payoff for those eight a.m. classes. Arts, psychology and social work? Not so much.[22]

Before I start hearing from indignant poli sci majors, let me say something in defense of a liberal education ("liberal" with a small *l*, as in a broad education, not a left-wing one). This kind of education has played an important part in America and in pursuing the American Dream. Our founders knew that we are born with the *right* to self-government but not the *tools* for self-government; these tools—the knowledge of history, government and our fellow man—must be taught. All education, be it at home or in elementary school, high school or college, should prepare Americans to be good citizens. And students with a passion for government or literature should follow that passion, but they also have a responsibility to understand the consequences. Let's be honest—Bill Murray was on to something when he laughed at

Andie MacDowell's degree in nineteenth-century French poetry in *Groundhog Day*. French poetry may be beautiful, even enlightening. But how useful is it when it comes time to get a job to pay back the loans it took to study Baudelaire?

With the responsibility of colleges and universities to deliver more educational bang for their hugely inflated buck comes the responsibility of students to make their education a wise investment. I was very encouraged when President Obama made this point during a visit to a manufacturing plant in Wisconsin early in 2014. He pointed out that we need to stop looking down on manufacturing and the skilled trades as lesser occupations. After all, he said, "Folks can make a lot more, potentially, with skilled manufacturing or the trades than they might with an art history degree."

But then, a few days later, when President Obama heard from some art history majors about this remark, he apologized for what he said. I thought that was kind of pathetic and I said so. The point he was making was an important and legitimate one. We no longer live in an economy in which most young people have the luxury of going deep into debt for an education that prepares them for an entry-level job at Starbucks. There's nothing wrong with being a coffeehouse server, of course; you just don't need to go into college loan debt to get the work.

The Department of Education reports that 10 percent of Americans whose student loans came due in 2011 were in default by 2013. Not acknowledging that the field of study chosen by the student has a role in the ability to pay back loans may spare some people's feelings, but it doesn't help anyone avoid a debt crisis.

Too many would-be students and their families are entering into one of the most significant investments they will ever make with little or no information on what to expect. What makes this situation all the more inexcusable is the fact that most colleges and universities already have the answers to the questions Americans have about the returns they can expect on their college investment. They're just not sharing it. To change this, I have teamed up with a Democrat, Senator Ron Wyden of Oregon, to propose the Student Right to Know Before You Go Act.

The idea is to create an online database—a Web site—of real, on-the-ground information for students and families to help them make smart decisions about their futures. Think a *U.S. News & World Report*–style ranking of all programs at all public and private degree-granting institutions, but with much more information about the graduation rates, average debt and starting salaries of students who go through them. With this database, students and their families could comparison shop. Thinking about a business program at College X? This database will show you if the cost is lower and the average wage higher at University Y. Or, after perusing the Web site, a student might decide to forego a business degree for a major that promises a better chance of landing a good job. In time, I can see this database becoming an essential reference, not only for students and their families, but for policy makers tasked with deciding where to invest taxpayer funds.

For other students—those who have already compiled a lot of debt—there is much more we can do to ease their burden and allow them to begin their lives. Today, students who have federal loans choose among repayment plans and their natural impulse is to get their loans paid off as soon as possible, which typically means they choose a monthly payment that is the same no matter how much they're making. The government offers repayment plans that are tied to income—if you're not making that much, you don't have to pay as much. There are actually four of these income-based plans, with confusingly alike-sounding names, with different eligibility criteria and repayment options. The whole system is so convoluted that few students use the income-based plans. And those brave souls who do attempt to use them too often get tangled in a slow and frustrating federal bureaucracy.

There is a better way for Americans struggling to pay off student debt. Government can and should make income-based repayment the default repayment method for anyone who takes out a student loan. When students sign the promissory note for a loan, they would automatically be enrolled in a repayment schedule based on income after graduation. If they're lucky and their income is high, they can make higher payments on a shorter schedule. If they find themselves in a lower-earning job—either by choice to give something back to the community or because entry level pays entry level wages—they will automatically make lower payments. Either way, it's a good deal for students and a good deal for taxpayers. Loan defaults would drop substantially, preserving students' credit and saving the taxpayers money.

Income-based repayment is an option I wish I had had when I graduated. My first job as a young attorney paid over $50,000 a year—more than my parents had ever made. I thought I was rich. But even though I was living with my parents, I was paying them rent. I was also trying to save for my wedding and to buy a house.

When the $1,500 student loan payments starting rolling in, I realized I couldn't pay them. And I was one of the lucky ones—*I had a job.*

So I did deferment. And forbearance. I paid only interest for a while. But the loans quickly became my single largest expense. I remember looking at the coupon book for one of them and realizing that at the pace I was paying these things, I wouldn't pay them off until I was over fifty. And sure enough, when I raised my right hand and was sworn in as a United States Senator in January 2011, I still owed over $100,000. It wasn't until the publication of my first book, *An American Son*, in 2012, that I was able to repay my loans.

That makes me a cautionary tale for young Americans like Evan. Evan is one of the lucky ones too—he landed his dream job working for the Miami Heat, but for now, at least, the job is entry level, part-time and doesn't pay that much. He's moved out of his parents' house and rents a place of his own, a single room in Miami, but he tries to be careful with his expenses—he always puts in for additional hours with the Heat and works a second job in retail. Still, Evan can't think about getting married or owning a home with his student debt hanging over his head. He works with people in their forties who are still paying off their undergraduate loans. Evan doesn't want that to be him in twenty years—he doesn't want to be *me* in twenty years.

"I don't want to have a family and be making payments on my kids' school while I'm still making payments on my school," he says. Still, he's afraid he might have to.

Right now, students like Evan are in a double bind: They are forced to assume all the risk of investing in higher education without having access to any data on the returns. The Student Right to Know Before You Go Act would help provide the data, and income-based repayment would help ease the process of repayment. Yet the current system of student loans still leaves Evan in debt just as he seeks to start his professional and personal life.

What if there were a way to give students the option of paying for their education without acquiring any student debt at all? What if investors assumed the risk that students and their families now bear alone in student loans? What if there were a way to finance your daughter's or son's higher education the way we finance start-up companies—by having others make the investment in their success?

There is a way and here is how it works. Let's say you are a student who needs $10,000 to pay for your last year of school. Instead of going into debt for $10,000, you could apply for a "Student Investment Plan" from a private investment group. These investment groups would pay your $10,000 tuition in return for a predetermined percentage of your income for a set period of time after graduation—maybe 4 percent of your income a year for ten years. At the end of that period, if the amount paid is greater than the investment, the investors make a profit. If it's less, they lose money. Either way, they assume the risk of paying for your education. Unlike with loans, you would be under no legal obligation to pay back that entire $10,000. Your only obligation would be to pay that 4 percent of your income per year for ten years, regardless of whether that ends up amounting to more or less than $10,000.

The idea of making investments in human capital traces back to the great economist Milton Friedman. But it was Ziggy Stardust himself, David Bowie, who provided the inspiration for such capital investing in college educations. In the late 1990s, Bowie sold shares of his pre-1990 albums' future sales revenues in order to raise cash. In return, true believers in the timelessness of "Fame" and "Space Oddity" received a percentage of his record sales and song royalties for ten years.

Bowie Bonds inspired some financial analysts who had watched promising classmates drop out of school because they couldn't afford to continue. What if students were, in effect, allowed to sell bonds in their future success? The concept has been tried in Europe and Latin America, where it has been a godsend to low-income students in particular. The practice—in which students sign contracts obligating them to the terms of the investment—hasn't been used much in the United States because there hasn't been legal clarity over the administration of the contracts. Questions of who would enforce the contracts, and state laws that prohibit the assignment of future income, have held back potential investors. But I believe it's time to take a more creative and innovative approach to paying for higher education.

The Investing in Student Success Act, which I introduced last year, paves the way for a new and less risky way for families to pay for college. The legislation creates investment savings accounts to allow investment groups, under carefully circumscribed rules to protect students, to invest in students' tuition in exchange for a piece of their postgraduation income. These groups would look at factors such as a student's major, the institution he or she attends and his or her academic record, and then assess the student's likelihood of getting a good job and paying them back.

The key to the success of this kind of investment is to create a large enough pool of students to spread the risk around. Some students will be good investments, others less so. For large employers, these education investments would provide a hedge against rising costs. Boeing, for example, could invest in engineering students. If, in the future, salaries for aeronautical and electrical engineers grew, Boeing would experience a higher return on its investment. Others will be attracted to make these investments for philanthropic reasons. But in the end it is the less advantaged students—the ones for whom traditional student loans would be the biggest burden—who would benefit the most.

Some critics have compared these kinds of contracts to indentured servitude, in which the purchaser literally owns the person and his labor in exchange for a payment or service. But that comparison is silly and inaccurate. My proposed law mandates that investors fully and clearly disclose the terms of the contract to students. It stipulates that the first $10,000 of the student's earnings each year after graduation must be exempt from the income total used to calculate repayment. That is, the first $10,000 cannot be included in the income from which a percentage is paid. In addition, the contract may not exceed 15 percent of the student's income in any given year, and the repayment period may not be longer than thirty years.

Student investment contracts won't replace student loans, nor should they. But they represent the kind of innovation we need to make higher education work for American families again. In addition to taking much of the risk out of paying for college, student investment contracts will give institutions new incentives to prepare students for the workplace. Investments in students' success would put the performance of higher education to the ultimate test: that of the marketplace.

Word will quickly get around in the investment community about which colleges and universities produce high-wage earners, giving all schools a new impetus to turn out students ready to succeed in the new economy.

———

Education's power to make the American Dream possible is something that is very close to me. First, admittedly, it was an abstraction my parents drilled into me as a child. Later, it became a reality that I saw change my sister's life. You see, I had the good fortune of being what we think of as a traditional student, coming out of high school and going immediately into a four-year degree program. My sister didn't have that luxury.

Barbara is my older sister. She never had the same opportunities I had. She married young and didn't go to college. Before my senior year in high school, she wound up living in our parents' home with an infant son and another on the way. All the odds were stacked against Barbara. She could have given up, put herself and her family in the hands of the social welfare system and passively accepted a life of dependence. But she didn't. In her early thirties she found herself working at an insurance company processing paperwork. She knew that if she didn't get a degree, she would never make a better life for her kids. So while my parents helped watch my nephews, Barbara went to Florida International University and earned an education degree. She went to work as a special education teacher. Then, while working as a teacher, she graduated with a master's degree in education. Today, she is the vice principal of an elementary school in Miami.

Barbara is a good example of what a twenty-first-century student looks like—not just the eighteen-year-old high school graduate but the older student. The struggling mom who wants to increase her earning potential but can't just drop everything and go back to school. The returning veteran. The worker who has lost a job that is never coming back and needs to be retrained. The high school student who wants to fix airplane engines but loses interest in schoolwork that seems geared toward the college-bound. It is a tragedy for these students of today that we still have an education system that caters to the students of yesterday.

There are millions of Americans who don't have the money, time or inclination to spend four to six years on a campus. At the same time, companies complain of a shortage of skilled workers. So smart, forward-looking companies are beginning to partner with local governments to close this gap. In Cleveland, General Electric worked with the city to create the MC2 STEM High School, which brings students to GE's manufacturing plant their sophomore year to get practical experience and mentoring from GE employees. MC2 STEM's graduation rate is 95 percent, compared with just 60 percent in the Cleveland public schools.[23]

These efforts deserve more of our support. Our education system—and we as a society—need to stop looking down our nose at people who don't sit behind a desk or a computer for a living. These are honest and, in many cases, well-paying jobs—jobs that are going unfilled for a lack of workers with the right skills. America has a shortage of welders, for instance, to fill new jobs in the oil and gas industry. Trade schools like the Hobart Institute of Welding Technology in Troy, Ohio, can't graduate skilled welders fast enough. Caterpillar is working with high schools and community colleges near its plants in North Carolina and Georgia to attract and train workers.[24]

There is no one-size-fits-all solution, but it is telling that so many of the solutions being offered are coming from businesses and the local governments that are eager to have them. In South Carolina, BMW has created an apprenticeship program with community colleges near its Spartanburg plant. The first class of BMW scholars graduated in 2012 with full-time jobs. Up in Brooklyn, IBM has partnered with New York City to create a hybrid technical school where students earn both high school and associate degrees when they graduate.

Like increasing numbers of students and parents, more and more businesses are surveying the value provided by American higher education and finding it wanting. A remarkable Gallup survey found that while a whopping 96 percent of college and university officials were confident that their institution was preparing students for the modern workforce, just 11 percent of business leaders strongly agreed.[25] The disconnect has gotten so bad that Google—the dream employer for the newly graduated—has begun to de-emphasize college credentials in hiring. And Peter Thiel, the cofounder of PayPal, is paying high school graduates *not* to go to college. What's wrong with this picture? And how do we fix it?

The widening gap between the cost of a college education and its utility in the modern economy has sparked a raging debate about whether we're sending too many young Americans to college today. Particularly with regard to the poorest Americans, a kind of fatalism has taken hold. We shouldn't fill their heads with dreams that they can't possibly achieve, some say. Not everyone is cut out for college, the pessimists add. And our system is encouraging students to go into debt pursuing college degrees when the odds are that they will not succeed.

There is truth here. There are good jobs that don't require a college degree—certainly not a traditional four-year degree from a residential college. And college *is* too expensive. Student debt *is* too high. But none of that argues for giving up on the dream of higher education that millions of American parents have for their children. It argues for transforming our current higher education system. Only a groundswell of creativity and technological change will lead to dramatic reductions in the time and expense of getting the education necessary to get ahead. That groundswell of creativity and innovation is possible if we have the political courage to bring it about.

American higher education today is an entrenched monopoly protected by government policy. Think Ma Bell before the breakup. Like all protected monopolies, colleges and universities set their own prices and are resistant to innovation and change. They use the power of government to keep competitors out and protect their monopoly power.

Education expert Andrew Kelly of the American Enterprise Institute tells the story of an experiment in online education that was killed by the higher education monopoly. In 2008, Tiffin University, a small private college in northwest Ohio, partnered with Internet start-up Altius to create Ivy Bridge College. The goal was to provide students with a flexible online associate degree that would be transferable to a number of cooperating four-year institutions. At less than half the cost of Tiffin's brick-and-mortar courses, the price was right. Ninety percent of Ivy Bridge students received Pell Grants. The program was a huge success. From just sixty-five students its first year of operation, enrollment exploded to sixteen hundred students by 2011. The next year, Ivy Bridge was honored with a Next Generation Learning grant from the Gates Foundation, one of only thirteen awarded nationwide. But one year later, in 2013, Ivy Bridge closed its virtual doors and went out of business.[26] What happened?

Before any institution of higher learning—be it a university, a community college or an online entity like Ivy Bridge—can be recognized as a degree-conferring institution, it has to be approved, or "accredited," by an independent regulatory board. There are six of these regional accreditation boards, each in charge of higher education institutions in different regions of the country. They were created after World War II for generally good reasons— chiefly to make sure that the flow of federal dollars under the GI Bill went to legitimate educational institutions. In the early 1950s, their role changed. From being a voluntary stamp of educational merit, accreditation became mandatory in order to receive federal financial aid. As federal aid grew, the power of the accreditation agencies grew. Their seal of approval eventually became the difference between life and death for colleges and universities.

In short, the accreditation agencies control the market for higher education. They decide which institutions get to call themselves a college or university or even offer a for-credit course. But, as Kelly notes, their power is based on a conflict of interest. Not only were these accreditation agencies created by existing colleges and universities, they are funded and staffed by them as well. They are like Coke and Pepsi getting together to determine who gets to sell soda. The result is that, when they review schools, they tend to favor established institutions and shut out competition from new, innovative and more affordable providers—providers like Ivy Bridge College. Although Ivy Bridge received initial high marks from its accreditation agency, the same agency shut it down after it showed signs of success. The Obama Department of Justice even got into the act, launching an investigation of Ivy Bridge for "false claims."[27]

At a time when technology should be transforming higher education, the accreditation process is standing in the way. There is a lot of excitement (not to mention anxiety) in the world of higher education about the potential of something that goes by the ungainly acronym MOOC. MOOC stands for "massive open online course," and these courses are now all over the place. For-profit companies like Coursera, Udacity and edX have been around for only a few years but have already attracted millions of users. These courses are filling an obvious need, but we still live in a world in which college credentials carry the day and colleges have zero incentive to grant credit for the successful completion of a MOOC as long as they are protected by the accreditation process. Even when colleges offer their own online courses, they charge brick-and-mortar prices to students learning from their living rooms. A *U.S. News & World Report* survey found that of four hundred colleges polled, 60 percent charge the same tuition for online courses as for in-person courses. Thirty-six percent charge more.[28] Why? *Because they can.*

Lessening the burden of student debt and finding innovative new ways to pay for college are important, but broad, innovative pathways to higher education for all Americans will not be found until we reform this broken and biased system. It's not rocket science. Free online learning is already a reality. Why couldn't a student, after completing an online course, test into college credit for it? She could pay a small fee to take a standardized test that, if passed, would allow the course to count toward a college degree. We already do this for high school students who take AP courses. They pass a test that allows them to count these courses toward their degree at most colleges.

To make "testing in" a reality at the college level, Congress could establish a new, independent accrediting board to ensure the quality of these free courses and make the credits transferable into the traditional system. The board would factor in input from the private sector and would allow students to qualify for some type of federal aid to cover any potential costs. By allowing online college courses to go toward a degree, we could create what would virtually amount to a debt-free college education.

First, though, we have to break the higher education monopoly. There are already some unique and powerful proposals for reform out there. Members of both parties are beginning to realize that for every day we delay bold accreditation reform, our education system leaves more Americans behind to languish in a dwindling market of low-skill jobs. Utah Senator Mike Lee has proposed allowing states to take control of the accreditation process. His proposal would ensure quality control in higher education while allowing the fifty states to compete for innovative and affordable educational institutions and online courses, even apprenticeships and technical programs that could count toward a degree. And to his credit, President Obama has also proposed changes to our higher education accrediting system.

We also need to take a cue from Google and look beyond our attachment to the college credential. There is a nearly infinite number of ways for an individual to learn and master a trade. We need to develop ways employers can easily recognize and trust to certify that individuals have certain skills.

For example, an aspiring cook may have mastered his or her craft from books and free online tutorials, or perhaps from the training of a parent who is a certified chef—or who simply cooks up a mean *ropa vieja* after years of preparing it for the family. These people should have the opportunity to prove their abilities and gain the certification necessary for employment without spending tens of thousands of dollars at a formal culinary school.

We could jump-start and create private sector confidence in this practice by creating a pilot program to hire such workers in federal agencies. The agencies would identify occupations where employees could have learned skills from nontraditional sources. The pilot program would then systematize the hiring of these individuals over a five-year period, allowing the results to be tracked and reported back to form the basis for future policy. We have little to lose and much to gain from finding new ways to connect Americans with good jobs.

I suspect we will find that, in many fields, the source of an employee's education is far less important than many previously thought. Those who have the skills and the aptitude to be successful in a job deserve the opportunity to be considered for employment, even if they learned the trade from a nontraditional source.

———

This new postindustrial economy offers great promise, but it has also created widespread economic insecurity. Millions live one broken-down car, one destructive storm, one serious illness away from financial collapse. People who have worked their whole lives in one industry have watched their jobs disappear. Parents are heartbroken knowing their children have done everything they were told they needed to do to succeed but now can't find a job in the field they studied for.

Our higher education system has long been hailed as the best in the world. It must be said that today, in many ways, we are coasting on that reputation. The fight for a quality higher education for all is the fight for the American Dream itself. It is the fight for the idea that no one should be held captive by the circumstances of his or her birth. Winning this fight should be among our most urgent priorities. At stake is our very identity as an exceptional nation.

More than that, at stake is the security of millions of families and the future of millions of young lives.

For Kristi, the University of Central Florida alumna who owes more today than the day she graduated, the frustration she feels about being in debt is overshadowed only by the guilt she feels about continuing to be a burden on her parents. She doesn't pay rent, but she helps out whenever she can. Still, she knows she's deferring their dreams as well. Both would like to retire, but they can't. Not now. Not until Kristi is able to start her life.

Chapter Five

ECONOMIC SECURITY IN AN INSECURE TIME

The Census Bureau has a great data visualization graphic that says a lot about who's winning and who's losing in America today. It's a map of the United States with lower-income counties in white and higher-income counties in green. A sliding bar across the bottom begins at $18,000 in median annual income and ends at over $110,000. As you slide the bar to the right and move into progressively higher income categories, the map turns from green to white. It's fascinating to watch. As the map becomes increasingly white, green islands of high income pop up along the coasts, around Chicago, a few good spots in Texas, of course. But when you've finished sliding the bar all the way to the top of the income scale, the whole country is white, with one small island of wealth— right smack on top of Washington D.C.[1]

While the rest of the country has been mired in the Great Recession and the Recovery That Wasn't, Washington D.C. has been booming. Thirteen of the thirty richest counties in America form a circle around Washington D.C.; six of the richest counties are directly adjacent to the nation's capital.[2] For the politicians, lobbyists, consultants, federal workers and contractors who live in these wealthy environs, life is pretty good. The price of the average house is on its way to a million dollars, restaurants are packed and yoga studios are plentiful. But what may be the biggest perk for the D.C. moneyed class is the fact that their children attend some of the best suburban public schools and private schools in the country. For their parents, school choice is a given. They have the means either to move to the right suburb near the right school or to pay the $20,000 to $30,000 annual tuition for a private school.

The same cannot be said for the residents of Washington D.C., who have been left behind by the big-government boom. Despite consistently spending more per student than almost anywhere else in the country, D.C.'s public schools are racked by violence and low achievement. Maybe that's why all recent presidents with school-age children (with the exception of Jimmy Carter) have exercised their choice and sent their kids to private schools. President Obama and Vice President Biden are no exception. Their children and grandchildren attend a private school in Washington whose tuition hovers around $30,000 a year.

To give D.C.'s poor and middle-class parents at least a shot at the choice of schools our leaders enjoy, in 2004 the GOP-led Congress created a federally funded scholarship called the D.C. Opportunity Scholarship. But President Obama and his allies in Congress have fought to kill the scholarship since he became president. For the past couple of years, supporters have managed to just barely maintain funding for the program despite the fact that recipients have shown academic gains and parents overwhelmingly love it.

At a time when income inequality is the topic of so much discussion in Washington, it's interesting, to say the least, that so much of the inequality being condemned coincides with proximity to government. And of course, it's not just an income divide; it's a power divide. There is a real disconnect between Washington D.C. and the average American county. More and more, it is the folks in the gleaming Capital City who are determining the fates of Americans in the struggling hinterlands. Kristeen is a typical example. She is a single mother of two who lives in Gainesville, Florida, far from the towering construction cranes that gild the nation's capital right now.

For Kristeen, getting by is an everyday, dawn-to-dusk, never-ending challenge. She has two young daughters: Lexi, who's six, and Jada, who's four. Because she has to work, day care is an absolute necessity. And at a cost of $235 a week, Kristeen says paying for it is like signing over her paycheck. It doesn't leave enough leftover for rent, her electric bill, car insurance, gas, food or any of her other daily expenses. So she's had to rely on government assistance. She is grateful for the help, but what she really wants is a better job so she can provide for herself and her two girls.

When Kristeen tucks her daughters in at night, she thinks about their futures. And she thinks about her own past. Growing up, she was never led to believe that an education was within her reach—some people even called her selfish when she enrolled in online classes to better herself after high school. Like so many parents, she's determined that her daughters have the things she never had. Not just the material things, but the independence she feels she has forfeited by being forced to accept government assistance. She wants Lexi and Jada to form their own strong opinions and convictions, to set goals for their futures and then act to achieve them, to be anything their dreams inspire them to be.

But something is looming on the horizon that causes Kristeen more anxiety than even her financial struggles. Soon Lexi and Jada will be forced to attend a public school that does not meet Kristeen's standards for their educations. It's nearby, but she knows it won't give them the education they need to escape the day-to-day grind that she deals with—a struggle she wants more than anything else for them to escape. This fact has left her feeling completely helpless. Kristeen doesn't know any wealthy or well-connected people. There are no Wall Street or Washington D.C. internships in Lexi's or Jada's future. And her job at a dog boarding facility brings in just $370 a week after taxes. Kristeen has no choice.

For millions of Americans like Kristeen, an economy that is not producing good jobs, an education system that is not preparing students for those jobs available, and poverty programs that trap people in dependence all come together in a very real daily struggle that transcends politics. It is simple math that dictates Kristeen's life, not campaign promises or ideological debates: How can she continue to make $370 a week and cover her bills and make a better future for her children? The answer is, she can't. She is not a victim, nor is she a "taker." She wants more than survival for her family. But no one in Washington of either party is helping her, least of all President Obama. He was elected on the promise that he stood with people like Kristeen but has presided over a system that has benefited the wealthy and connected.

When conservatives talk about policies that will create jobs, promote economic growth and increase opportunity for Americans, we often start with tax reform—and for good reason. Our tax code is too complicated, punishes productivity and is full of loopholes and carve-outs created by special interests. A simpler tax code with lower tax rates would do more than just about anything else to create jobs and unleash America's potential.

But when *reform* conservatives consider the tax code, we see the need to do all these things and more. The most important cultural and economic institution in America—the family—doesn't have lobbyists on Capitol Hill; it doesn't have lawyers pressuring government for special treatment. And you know what they say about tax policy in Washington: If you're not at the table, you're on the menu. So it's no surprise that our tax code actively discriminates against families raising children. In all our justified talk of tax reform, conservatives have emphasized pro-growth policies but somehow overlooked pro-family policies. We need to do both.

The case for a tax code that is both pro-growth and pro-family plays out in millions of homes of parents raising children every day. Americans like Kristeen are doing something more than raising their children; they're making an investment in all of our futures. They're bearing the enormous cost of raising the next generation—the children who will be the taxpayers of tomorrow and who will support the generational entitlements like Social Security and Medicare that we all benefit from.

Before there were retirement security programs, people depended on their children to take care of them in old age. Today, with Social Security and Medicare, the incentive to rely on children for retirement security is less. For some people, it's nonexistent. They can afford to have no children and still know that our retirement security programs will be there for them. That's okay. But it's parents raising children who are producing the taxpayers who will pay for those entitlements, and that costs money. Our tax code, however, doesn't account for this investment. The result is parents effectively pay into our generational entitlement programs twice: first when they pay their own taxes, and second when they pay to produce the next generation of taxpayers. Utah Senator Mike Lee, with whom I have worked to produce a new, pro-growth, pro-family tax plan, calls this feature of our current tax code the "parent tax penalty."

Take the example of two families, one with children and one without. Say they earn the same incomes and pay the same amount in payroll taxes to support Social Security and Medicare. Both receive identical benefits, but the couple with children also has to spend $300,000 per child (the government's lowball estimate of raising a child, which doesn't include child care, college or the wages many moms forego to raise children). It's these children, as future taxpayers, who will eventually pay for the benefits received by both families. The difference between the investment made and the benefits received is the parent tax penalty.

The plan Senator Lee and I have proposed would restore some

semblance of fairness to our tax code for families raising children by recognizing the investment they make. It would simplify the tax code by consolidating the current seven income tax brackets into just two: 15 percent and 35 percent. However, the centerpiece of the plan is a new $2,500 tax credit for each child under sixteen. The current code offers a $1,000 per child tax credit that phases out at higher incomes, as well as a tax deduction for each dependent child, which just reduces the amount of your taxable income. Our new tax credit will actually reduce the amount of taxes owed by $2,500 for each child. The sum of this expanded Child Tax Credit is limited to the total of income and payroll tax liabilities and it is charged after all other tax liabilities and after all other tax credits. This design is intended to offset the payroll tax liability of parents, because payroll taxes finance the entitlement system.

Not only would this plan have the American virtue of treating all taxpayers more equally, it would provide real, immediate relief to middle- and working-class parents. With these reforms, a married couple with two children who make the median national income of $51,000 would get a tax cut of about $5,000 per year. That's not enough to pay for braces and summer camp, but it is a nice offset to the cost of day care to allow a mom to work more hours, or to compensate for lost wages so she can work less.

Some critics on the right have argued that cutting marginal tax rates and the payroll tax instead would have bigger pro-growth effects on our economy. There are at least two answers to this. The first is that the Child Tax Credit is but one part of the broader Lee-Rubio pro-growth tax reform plan that will reduce tax rates for individuals and businesses, end special interest tax loopholes and dramatically simplify the tax code. As I describe in Chapter Two, businesses would pay a lower flat tax and have the ability to expense or immediately write off the cost of every investment they make in their company. The Lee-Rubio plan would also eliminate the double taxation of capital gains and dividend income. These pro-growth reforms would increase productivity, unleash economic growth and raise real wages for middle-class workers.

In addition, the Lee-Rubio reforms have the virtue of being achievable. There are good pro-growth economic cases to be made for a flat tax or lowering marginal rates even further instead of offering a new child credit. But at a time when corporate profits are reaching record highs and wages are stagnating,[3] I know of no plausible political scenario in which such reforms could be enacted by Congress. Our pro-growth, pro-family tax plan, in contrast, is realistic and achievable. Our plan combines pro-family and pro-growth tax changes that can be embraced by all Americans—and actually made into law.

Another criticism concerning tax plans that reduce or even eliminate the tax burden of some Americans is that they will increase calls for more government spending because fewer Americans are having to bear the costs. This line of reasoning is reminiscent of the "47 percent" controversy in which Mitt Romney's opponents accused him of casting a large portion of Americans as "takers" who want big government but don't want to have to pay for it.

There is some intuitive logic to the idea that reducing the tax rolls while expanding government benefits is a bad idea. People who never expect to see their income—and thus their taxes—go up could be tempted to support more government spending. But providing tax relief for parents raising children is a very different proposition. As former U.S. Treasury official Robert Stein put it, our plan "does not simply reduce the tax rolls based on income. Instead, it reduces the tax rolls based on *parenting*" (emphasis mine).[4] Of course, raising children is a temporary condition—although lots of folks with grown children still living in their basements might disagree with me. Children grow up, parents lose the tax credit and their taxes go up. Parents know this, which means they are less likely to support more government spending while their taxes are—temporarily—reduced.

In the meantime, our pro-family, pro-growth tax plan gives parents relief when they most need it: when their expenses are high because they're raising children. Stein argues, in fact, that reducing the cost of raising children by temporarily lowering their taxes may make parents *less* likely to support more government spending. His point makes sense. When parents face expenses raising children that they can't meet, they look to government to fill in the gap. Stein claims that the number of Americans who would support government-funded preschool, for example, would be smaller if parents had the means to pay for more day care.

If you ask me, the better—not to mention more conservative—option is to allow parents to keep more of their own money and make their own choices, rather than have government spend more of our own money and make choices for us.

I've talked to and heard from middle- and lower-class Americans from all walks of life in the course of developing my conservative reform agenda. It was the rare person who didn't have a story of how the Affordable Care Act had either increased their costs or limited their health care options—or both. Time and again, the impact of the law has been described as gratuitously adding even more hardship to already struggling families. Families who were perfectly happy with their coverage described being forced to pay more for coverage they didn't want or need. Some, like the Broyles family in Chapter Two, have been forced out of the health insurance system altogether and sought refuge in faith-based cost-sharing plans. I've heard plenty of horror stories about dealing with the Affordable Care Act Web site. One family described Obamacare officials repeatedly demanding that they provide pay stubs from their children before the family could enroll for health insurance. Their kids are twelve, ten and five.

After the first enrollment period for coverage under the law ended last year, the administration and its allies in the media did their best to convince us that the law had become a stunning success. In fact, when judged against all the promises the president himself made for the law, it has been a stunning failure. Here's what the president said when he came before Congress to lobby for the law in September 2009:

> It will provide more security and stability to those who have health insurance. It will provide insurance for those who don't. And it will slow the growth of health care costs for our families, our businesses and our government.[5]

The Affordable Care Act has failed each of these promises. Those who have health insurance have seen their premiums go up. Enrollees in the health care exchanges have been older, sicker and more expensive to insure, forcing rates up for everyone. When ten states submitted their proposed health insurance premiums for this year, the companies that insure the most people in all but one of the states proposed increasing premiums between 8.5 percent and 22.8 percent.[6] Premiums are going up almost 14 percent for one of Arizona's most popular plans.[7] In another populous state, Ohio, premiums are set to increase by 13 percent this year.[8] In Iowa, rates are slated to climb by a similar amount.

The picture that emerges from the many people I've heard from is that, instead of helping struggling middle- and working-class Americans afford health insurance, the Affordable Care Act is actually pricing these Americans out of the health insurance market. Middle-income folks talk about being caught between a rock and a hard place: making too much money to qualify for subsidies under the law, but making too little to be able to afford the higher prices. The data back this up.

At the close of last year's enrollment period, the Department of Health and Human Services released a report showing that the overwhelming majority of Americans who signed up for Obamacare received significant government subsidies to pay for their insurance. Of the 6.8 million people who actually paid for the insurance they signed up for, a full 5.9 million received subsidies—big ones, an average of $264 a month.[9] But for those Americans who are not eligible for subsidies—and even those who qualify only for smaller subsidies—the higher premiums, higher deductibles and narrower choices of doctors caused by the law are not working. One health insurance expert, Bob Laszewski, put it this way: "The Obamacare plans are unattractive to all but the poorest, who get the biggest subsidies and the lowest deductibles. The working class and middle class are not getting access to attractive benefits."[10]

On the other end of the income spectrum are higher-income Americans, who, along with many of the top doctors, are rushing to join concierge, or cash-only, health networks in order to avoid the regulations and restrictions imposed by the Affordable Care Act. What's taking shape as a result is a three-tiered health care system in which the poorest are subsidized in Obamacare, the richest can afford the best private networks and the middle class is left out in the cold. In fact, far from reducing the number of uninsured, the law threatens to create what Laszewski calls "a chronically uninsured class" of middle-class and working-class Americans. It's not difficult to predict what happens next if supporters of the law continue to hold sway in Washington. As reporter Byron York has written, the next act for Obamacare is likely to be calls in Washington to expand subsidies to the working and middle classes to compensate for the higher costs created by the law.

The abject failure of the Affordable Care Act—visible to all but the administration's most ardent true believers—has tempted some of my colleagues to sit back and allow the law to collapse of its own weight, bringing its supporters down with it. This may or may not be good politics—that's not the point. What I know is that it would be a huge disservice to the American people to allow our health care system to collapse just to make a political point. Already, Obamacare is doing damage, not just to our health care system but to our economy as a whole. At a time when those who want a job can't find one and record numbers of young men have opted out of the workforce altogether, the law is actively discouraging work. Employers are being forced to cut hours and avoid hiring workers. And employees are falling further into the poverty trap I discussed in Chapter Three. The more they earn, the less of a subsidy they receive, so the less they work. The effect, according to the Congressional Budget Office, will be the equivalent of 2.5 million people simply stopping working by 2024.[11]

Another, lesser-known danger in Obamacare is that it contains a bailout for big insurance companies. The legislation originally contained "risk corridors" for insurance companies that limit the expenses they are liable for—basically insuring the insurers against unanticipated major losses. Under normal circumstances, risk corridors can be a good thing. They protect consumers against disruptions in service. And when they are budget neutral—that is, when they don't expose taxpayers to open-ended risk—they can even protect taxpayers against being on the hook for losses if something unforeseen happens.

The problem with the Affordable Care Act—one of the many problems—is that its failures aren't unanticipated or unforeseen; they are virtually written into the law. As many predicted, the law has pushed premium prices upward. The exchanges aren't competitive markets—they're more like high-risk pools—and their prices are reflecting that. The losses facing insurance companies under the law aren't the result of one or two of them miscalculating their rates. They're being felt across the board. The entire industry is being primed for a bailout.

A few months after the law went into effect, the Obamacare risk corridors went from being a badly needed insurance policy to what one writer called an Obama administration "slush fund" for the insurance companies. Remember when, in November 2013, President Obama was forced to announce that Americans whose insurance policies had been banned by Obamacare could keep them? The president's infamous "If you like your plan you can keep it" promise had turned out to be a cruel joke and millions of people were being forced off their insurance plans. To avoid political Armageddon, the president unilaterally declared that they could keep their plans. That meant that millions of healthier, lower-cost Americans who were supposed to be forced onto the exchanges weren't, and that was bad news for the insurance companies. The American Academy of Actuaries predicted that the move would result in higher than expected costs for the insurance companies and therefore higher costs for the federal government through the risk corridors. Despite creating these higher costs, however, the Obama administration has done nothing to change the risk corridors. The effect has been to put the American taxpayers on the hook for the insurance companies' higher costs.

Last year, I introduced legislation to prevent this bailout. My office was quickly inundated with calls from health insurance executives begging us to back off. They claimed that without the bailout they would have to raise premiums dramatically. Without it, they pleaded, they could no longer participate in the exchanges. Their message was clear: Removing the bailout provision would be to punish them for the errors of Obamacare.

What the insurance executives never mentioned, though, was

how hard many of them had lobbied for the law when it was first debated. After all, the individual mandate would force people to become their customers and the bailout would protect them from losses. So they used their power and access to have Obamacare written in a way beneficial to them. And now to keep them in line, they're getting a taxpayer bailout. It's classic crony capitalism.

That is why it is imperative that we repeal Obamacare and that we not waste time in doing so. The law is a disaster that puts affordable health care out of reach of more middle-class Americans every day it is in effect. It's not too late to replace it with reforms that give all Americans the chance to buy the kind of health insurance they want, from any company they choose, at a price they can afford. Wisconsin Representative Paul Ryan and I have proposed a set of modern, market-based health care reforms we believe will do just that. At the heart of our plan are two simple changes to our health care system that will make health care more affordable and ensure that every American gets the same benefit, regardless of where they live or where they work.

The first change is to convert the tax preference for employer-sponsored health care into a tax credit for the individual. The current system allows employers to deduct their share of the cost of their employees' health care as a business expense. It also has employees deduct the costs of their health insurance from their gross income. The result has been to favor employer-provided health care. This third-party payer system, in which the consumer doesn't control his or her own health care, encourages health care consumption and drives up costs. But health care isn't free. The higher costs to employers have resulted in lower wages for employees.

Our tax credit, in contrast, would restore the middle class's ability to both afford and control their own health care. If everyone under sixty-five who is not on Medicaid participated, we could offer a $2,000 credit for an individual plan and a $5,800 credit for a family plan—more than enough to cover the average worker's current out-of-pocket costs. Americans could use the credit to purchase whatever insurance plan they want or deposit it in a Health Savings Account (HSA). What's more, the credit would be refundable—if an individual's health care costs are less than the credit, they get to keep the difference. It would be paid out every month, just like a health care premium. And in an era when the average worker stays at a job for less than five years, it would travel from job to job with the individual.

In order to safeguard those employers and employees who prefer the old system, our second reform, such as it is, is to maintain the ability of employers to deduct their health care costs as a business expense. This will ensure that some employers still have an incentive to provide health insurance to their employees. Our plan would phase out the employer health insurance exclusion over ten years, while immediately creating a refundable health care tax credit. This would ensure the creation of a vibrant individual health insurance marketplace while avoiding disruptions to the health insurance plans that people currently receive from their employers.

In addition to changing the tax treatment of health insurance, the Ryan-Rubio plan would increase access to low-cost health care options like HSAs, increase the bargaining power of small business, reform medical liability to decrease the practice of defensive medicine and allow people to purchase health insurance across state lines. To provide a better option than Obamacare to protect the most vulnerable, our plan would support the creation of state-based high-risk pools for those with preexisting conditions who can't get coverage in the private market.

The high cost of making ends meet today hits one group particularly hard: single parents, particularly our more than ten million single mothers. Many of these women have been abandoned by the father of their children. All, like Kristeen, face the struggles of parenthood alone. In the last chapter of this book, I will have more to say about how difficult it is for single parents to achieve the American Dream, and what we as a society can do about it. But for now we have to face the fact that we have a lot of Americans like Kristeen, most of whom want a better life for themselves and especially for their children.

Kristeen knows that the only chance she has of realizing her dream for her daughters is to get a better job. Not just a job that pays more, but also one with some flexibility in its work hours so she can make it to parent-teacher conferences or stay home from work when one of the girls is sick. And she knows that the only chance she has of getting a better job is by earning a degree.

So Kristeen enrolled in online classes in early childhood education, which she hoped would lead to a job that not only paid more but also allowed her to be with her daughters after school. But it cost around $1,200 per class—much more than the cost of physically attending the local community college. With all her other expenses, she couldn't afford it, so she dropped out.

For parents who are working, the government provides a $1,000 per child tax credit, called the Child and Dependent Care Tax Credit, to help offset the cost of child care. The problem is, under today's outdated system, a single mom like Kristeen loses her eligibility for the credit if she quits working and returns to school full-time.

In today's job market, this is a self-defeating rule that keeps people like Kristeen trapped in dead-end jobs. Kristeen would like to become a teacher so she can be at home more with her daughters. Our policies should support, not hinder, her ambition. That's why I have proposed allowing parents who are pursuing their education to be eligible for the child care credit too.

Kristeen will tell you that as important as her own education is to her, the education of her children is her greatest priority. Yet, unless something changes dramatically in Kristeen's life, her daughters will be headed to an underperforming school. She desperately wants them to have a better education than she received, but she feels completely helpless to do anything about it. We should empower all parents to have a choice of schools for their children. To do this, I've proposed a federal tax credit that encourages contributions to scholarship organizations, which would distribute private school scholarships to children like Jada and Lexi.

Louisiana Governor Bobby Jindal likes to say that the American Dream begins with education. He should know. Against the active opposition of the Obama Department of Justice, Jindal has fought for good schools for the poorest kids in Louisiana through school choice. When Hurricane Katrina ripped through New Orleans in 2005, it literally washed away the corrupt, underperforming public school system there. What has been built in the aftermath is a demonstration project for the transformative power of empowered parents and motivated teachers. When school began last fall, the New Orleans Recovery School District became the first in the country to consist of all charter schools. Graduation rates are up by over 20 percent since before Katrina. The number of children performing at grade level in reading and math has more than doubled since 2007.[12]

There is no reason that poor parents like Kristeen should have to send their children to a failing school just because it happens to be down the street. Rich people exercise their school choice, either by sending their kids to private schools or by moving to neighborhoods with good public schools. Our leaders can no longer be allowed to get away with telling us they care about the poor while they stand in the way of empowering parents to choose the best school for their children. A quality education is more important than ever, because the jobs of tomorrow will require more education and skills than ever before. Any so-called leader who stands between parents and the school of their choice is consigning another generation of American children to poverty, plain and simple.

In earlier chapters, I discussed other reforms to our outdated, big-government institutions that will help Americans like Kristeen with the daily struggle to make ends meet. For instance, she had the right idea when she sought an online education. Yet she discovered a perplexing truth: All the resources of the Web still haven't managed to bring down the cost of a degree. The online classes she wanted to take actually cost more than going to school in person. The reason higher education institutions have been able to get away with this is that they are effectively a cartel that can squash competition by lower-cost providers.

I have proposed that Congress break up this cartel by creating a new, independent entity to encourage the development of affordable and accessible online options for folks like Kristeen. I've proposed ways to empower her to acquire employable training from the resources all around her—including free online tools, apprenticeships, mentorships and personal training.

I've also proposed a transformation of how we fight poverty in America. We've seen time and again that effective antipoverty programs—the kind that incentivize work, bolster training and education, and open up transformative opportunities—come from the states, which know the specific needs of their people far better than Washington. We need to transfer our federal antipoverty spending to the states. And to further encourage work, we should create the Wage Enhancement Credit, which would raise Kristeen's wage at the pet kennel. Much more effectively than a minimum wage, such a wage credit would make work pay for Kristeen without killing jobs for other workers.

The paradox of the American Dream is that it evokes such grand, stirring passion, but it is in reality the sum of the mundane details of life. It's a car payment you can make, the mortgage you can afford, the college acceptance letter your daughter receives in the mail. Whether the American Dream is achievable has a real impact on real people's lives.

Our success as a nation isn't measured simply by the size of our economy or the performance of our stock market. Instead, it depends on whether Americans like Kristeen are able to go back to school, get a better job and give their children a better life. These are small things in the sweep of history, but big things in the course of people's lives. How we choose to address them will define our legacy. And it will define Kristeen's future.

Chapter Six

RETIREMENT IN YOUR OWN TIME, ON YOUR OWN TERMS

My mother turned eighty the day I was elected to the United States Senate. I remember looking at her on election night in the courtyard of the Biltmore Hotel, standing on the stage with me, confetti filling the air around us. I choked up with emotion at just the sight of her. She had dreamed of being an actress, but had spent her life in hard work—mostly as a maid—to give my brother and sisters and me the opportunities she never had. That night, she had been a widow less than two months. Before we lost my father, he had spent a lifetime sacrificing along with her for me to be up there on that stage.

My parents never earned enough to save much for retirement or to earn a pension. They both worked well past retirement age, and when they couldn't work anymore, it was Social Security and Medicare that allowed them to retire in comfort and security. They are two of the hardest-working people I have ever known, but when the time came, they counted themselves blessed to have come to a country where a life of hard work could be rewarded with a dignified retirement.

Mom is still with me, living with my sister and her husband in the house she and my father purchased in 1985. At eighty-four, her health is declining, but, thanks to Social Security, Medicare and the love of a caring daughter, her life is about as good as it can be.

Spending time with her and my sister Barbara and her husband, Orlando, never fails to remind me how lucky we are. My mother has her benefits, and my siblings and I have the time and the resources to care for her. But lately, more and more Americans aren't so lucky. For millions of us, financial security has faded—and with it, any hope of a stable and secure retirement. Americans at or near retirement increasingly live in fear for what the future holds. Like my parents, they have reached the sunset of their lives in the United States of America. But unlike my parents, they are nearing retirement uncertain and insecure about what the future holds.

Joyce is one of those Americans. She's almost sixty-four and her husband, Scott, is seventy-five. All their lives, they've played by the rules. "We've always worked, paid our bills and tried to do things the right way—like we were taught was the right way," she says. When Scott retired over a decade ago, he invested about $80,000 of his pension in the stock market and lost it. Then Joyce got downsized—"displaced" was the euphemism her employer used, as if she were a set of car keys—from her job at a newspaper. She got another job at another newspaper and was downsized again. After running through their savings, Joyce's COBRA ran out and she found herself without health insurance. When she had what she calls "some health problems"—her fourth heart attack and rheumatoid arthritis, to be exact—the bills had to go on credit cards. Then they had to sell the house they had lived in for fourteen years. They didn't make a penny on the sale. They just felt lucky to have gotten out from under the mortgage.

"So here we sit, with virtually nothing," Joyce says. Less than nothing, actually. She calculates they owe over $20,000 in credit card bills. She has reached the point where she has contacted one of those companies that is supposed to negotiate with the credit card companies to reduce your monthly payment. She's not optimistic, but what can she do? The credit cards were her only form of payment when she was unemployed.

"You need gas in your car and you gotta do something or pretty soon you're not going to have a job again," she says. "It's like a circle."

The most work Joyce can find is part-time administrative duty at the chamber of commerce. Scott picks up a few hours now and then with an auto dealership. When asked if she had hoped to be retired by now, Joyce erupts in bitter laughter. They had wanted to buy a mobile home and travel the country. "I don't see that happening now," she says. She's still uninsured—she refused to buy insurance under the Affordable Care Act—so she is holding her breath until she qualifies for Medicare. In the meantime, health problems be damned, she has no choice but to work.

It's those words—"no choice"—that seem to define Joyce and Scott these days. They've been left at the end of long working lives with no good options. They have no choice but to keep working. They had no choice but to sell their house. No choice but to run up their credit card debt. And the future doesn't look like it will be offering any more freedom.

"I don't know what's down the road. We just live from day to day. We do what we gotta do. Sometimes it's not easy," Joyce says, "but I have no choice."

———

Americans like Joyce, Scott and my mom were on my mind last spring when I spent a fine May afternoon outlining a plan to re-form our retirement system to an audience at the National Press Club in Washington D.C. Washington has a long and dishonor-able tradition of attacking anyone who dares say what everyone knows is true: that Americans are more insecure about their retire-ment than at any time in the past eighty years. Personal savings were decimated by the financial collapse and recession. Economic stagnation has endangered pensions. And most threatening of all to Washington politicians: Americans' retirement savings of last resort—Social Security and Medicare—are nearing bankruptcy.

Financial analysts like to use the analogy of a three-legged stool when they talk about saving for retirement. Today, each of the three legs of our traditional retirement stool—personal sav-ings, pensions and Social Security—is wobbling. And if we do nothing, each of the three will likely cease to exist as we know them well before my generation enters retirement.

The instability of each of the three traditional sources of retire-ment savings is caused by a variety of factors, yet they all share one common cause of decay: the lack of sustained economic growth. Economic stagnation prevents wages from keeping pace with costs, affecting the ability of the middle class to save. It also affects the ability of states and companies to fulfill their pension promises. And as earnings stall and unemployment and underemployment spread, it contributes to the erosion of the tax revenue needed to finance Social Security and Medicare.

These are facts—not theories or partisan talking points. Yet there appears to be no urgency in Washington about doing something about the looming retirement crisis. On the contrary, too many politicians lie in wait for their opponents to dare to raise these truths so they can pounce. When Wisconsin Representative Paul Ryan suggested a plan to shore up Medicare a few years ago, his opponents put out an ad featuring a Paul Ryan look-alike actually pushing an elderly lady in a wheelchair off a cliff. That's the kind of subtlety and reason that has attended this debate.

That day last spring, I had no doubt that my suggestions would be used against me to try to convince seniors that I was trying to take away the benefits they had worked so hard for. Politics is politics. But I went ahead despite the likely partisan onslaught for two reasons. The first, I admit, is pretty selfish: *My mother depends on Medicare and Social Security.* I love my mother. Simply put, I would never support anything that would hurt her or retirees like her.

The second reason is less close to home but, at least for me, equally undeniable. Social Security is our largest domestic program and the largest source of income for most retirees. Medicare is the indispensable health care lifeline for the nation's seniors. But an aging population, the sluggish economy and chronic fiscal irresponsibility in Washington have combined to doom these programs if nothing changes. The most recent Medicare Trustees Report predicts that the Social Security disability trust fund will be bankrupt in late 2016—*late next year*—and the retirement fund will be insolvent in 2034. Medicare will be bankrupt by 2030. These facts lead to one inescapable conclusion: *Anyone who is in favor of doing nothing about Social Security and Medicare is in favor of bankrupting Social Security and Medicare.* The politicians who so fiercely defend the status quo—and attack anyone who questions it—have it exactly wrong.

As you can no doubt tell, America's retirement crisis is something I feel strongly about, and something I've been thinking about for some time. In fact, I've come to believe the single most important step we can take to relieve the retirement insecurity of Americans is to control government spending and spur economic growth. Everything I've talked about in this book so far—from making college more affordable to encouraging work to making America the best place in the world to invest and innovate—is aimed at restoring the American Dream by creating dynamic economic growth. Unless and until all Americans can earn more and save more, retirement will remain an uncertain—even unattainable—prospect for too many of us. No plan to avert a retirement crisis will work without robust and sustained economic growth in the years to come.

But while economic growth is essential to ease retirement insecurity, it's not enough. The Broyles family is a good example of why. After having several jobs, Daniel and Becky are in business for themselves today. They don't have any company pension or retirement plan. What's more, they are likely to live longer than their parents or grandparents did. They love their work selling home furnishings and have no plans to retire.

More and more workers in our modern postindustrial economy are like the Broyleses. Instead of working at one company for life the way our parents and grandparents did, most of us today will have a number of jobs over the course of our working life. Many of these jobs won't offer retirement plans. What's more, the average American worker is now living and voluntarily working longer than Franklin Delano Roosevelt ever could have imagined when he came up with Social Security. Not only do we need to have economic growth to avert a retirement crisis, our retirement programs need to be modernized and restructured to meet the needs of a new kind of American worker. So our first challenge is to make it easier for these American workers to save more and work longer.

Albert Einstein is reported to have once said that the most powerful force in the universe is compound interest. Nowhere is this truer than with saving for retirement. The best way for Americans to guarantee security in retirement is to gradually build a nest egg of savings, starting as early in life as possible. Social Security was never meant to be the sole source of retirement income. For Americans of my generation and younger, this will be especially true. As the number of workers supporting retirees in our system declines, it will become more and more necessary for people to have adequate private savings.

But retirement can seem a long way off when you can't afford to pay your mortgage or save for your children's education. A reported three quarters of Americans today are living paycheck to paycheck with little or no savings for an immediate need like a job loss or medical emergency.[1] When you're cutting it this close, saving for retirement can be almost impossible. In fact, a recent survey found that over a third of Americans have less than $1,000 saved for retirement.[2] This problem is particularly acute in minority households. Three out of four black families and four out of five Latino families have less than $10,000 in retirement savings. That is in contrast to one out of two white families. One reason? Only 54 percent of black and Asian workers and 38 percent of Latino workers have an employer-sponsored retirement plan.[3]

In addition to stagnating wages, another reason for the growing retirement savings crisis is the nature of work today. Throughout much of the last century, you could leave school and go to work at a local company or factory, stay there for the next forty or fifty years, and then retire with a pension. Today the average worker stays at each job for only about four and a half years—and that's only the *average* worker. An astounding 91 percent of the millennial generation say they expect to be in each job for only two or three years, a vocational restlessness that translates into fifteen to twenty different jobs over the course of a career.[4]

Add to that the fact that many jobs, particularly low-wage ones, don't have employer-sponsored retirement plans. Seventy-five million Americans—mostly part-time employees of small businesses, women and minorities—are working for employers that do not offer a retirement plan.[5] And the rapidity with which Americans change employers these days virtually guarantees that those who do have access to an employer plan won't for their full career. Some are never told about the existence of a plan or just choose not to go through the hassle of enrolling. It's no wonder, then, that so many Americans have a fatalistic attitude about saving for retirement. A full 80 percent of people ages thirty to fifty-four believe they won't have enough in the bank when it comes time to retire.[6]

Americans are rapidly on their way to giving up on saving for their retirement. Instead of spending their time trying to find Paul Ryan look-alikes to shove old ladies off cliffs, more politicians in Washington should be asking themselves why this is and what can be done about it. Instead of attacking anyone who dares question the status quo, Washington might stop to think about how retirement programs originally built for workers who had one job in their lifetime can conceivably be expected to meet the needs of workers who will have ten.

I think one reason members of Congress aren't sweating the retirement savings issue too much is because they have one of the most efficient employer-sponsored savings plans in America. Members of Congress and other federal employees have exclusive access to the Thrift Savings Plan (TSP). Like a traditional employer-sponsored 401(k), the TSP allows federal employees to save pretax money for retirement. But unlike the typical employer-sponsored plan, it charges fees that are a fraction of those charged by most private defined-contribution plans and offers high rates of return. When costs are lower and returns are higher, beneficiaries save more. So the twisted irony is that members of Congress—who are employees of the citizens of the United States—have access to a superior savings plan, while many of their employers—the American people—are often left with access to no plan at all.

The most obvious and most just solution, I believe, is to give Americans who don't have access to an employer-sponsored plan the option of enrolling in the federal Thrift Savings Plan. Giving Americans hard at work in the private sector who lack a retirement savings plan the same one that members of Congress enjoy can be done at little cost—the infrastructure is already in place. These private employees wouldn't be offered matching funds, so the only expense involved would be the additional administrative costs of handling the new deposits.

The workers who are most likely not to be offered retirement plans by their employers are younger and lower income—precisely the Americans who most need new incentives to save. Conservatives have long pointed to the Thrift Savings Plan as the gold standard when proposing new ways for Americans to save for retirement. Now is the time for us to act to give Americans more options to save. Opening Congress's retirement plan to the American people will allow us to bring the prospect of a secure, comfortable and independent retirement into reach for millions of people.

Giving Americans more options to save is the first part of solving the retirement security puzzle. The next part is ensuring that older workers have the ability to work as long as they want or need without being punished for it. And that brings us back to Joyce.

A couple of years ago, out of sheer desperation, Joyce elected to begin receiving Social Security benefits early, at sixty-two, while she was still working. But because of something called the Retire-ment Earnings Test, which penalizes workers who claim their ben-efits early while they still have jobs, Joyce estimates she's receiving $300 a month less than she would if she had waited until she was sixty-five to claim her benefits.

The Retirement Earnings Test is like a 50 percent tax levied on the earnings of older workers—a tax on top of the payroll tax they already pay to finance Social Security. It works by reducing bene-fits by approximately fifty cents for every dollar a person between the ages of sixty-two and sixty-five earns in excess of $15,000 a year. Someone like Joyce has no choice but to pay this tax—she had to keep working and accept the cut to her benefits. But other Americans who have the option not to work usually stop working when they get to be sixty-two for no other reason than to avoid paying this penalty.

The Retirement Earnings Test is as old as Social Security itself. It was born of a Depression-era impulse on the part of Washington to create jobs for younger workers by encouraging older workers to retire. Today, eighty years later, in a radically transformed econ-omy with retirement savings at historic lows, it's still providing a disincentive for seniors to work. What is even more nonsensical about this policy is that it doesn't save any money. When a senior hit by this tax finally reaches sixty-five, his or her benefits are hiked way up to make up for any loss caused by the Retirement Earnings Test. The benefits received end up being mostly the same. This is good news for Joyce, but bad news for the older Americans who, not realizing their benefits will come back up to compensate, quit working to avoid the tax.

A 2014 Merrill Lynch study found that almost three out of four Americans over fifty say their ideal retirement includes some kind of work.[7] And that's their *ideal*—to continue to do what they love, or start a new chapter with some new balance of work and leisure. Other older Americans will have no choice but to work past retirement. In either case, to avoid punishing them, we should eliminate the Retirement Earnings Test altogether. It's another low-cost, high-impact move we can make to ease the retirement crisis. One economist estimates that abolishing the tax would raise employment among early retirees by 5.3 percent, a significant increase for a reform that has no long-term budgetary cost.[8]

Another tax that provides a powerful disincentive for older Americans to continue to work is the 12.4 percent payroll tax itself. As the tax code is currently written, those who keep working past retirement age continue to pay Social Security taxes while receiving almost no extra benefits in return. The Social Security benefit is calculated based on a worker's highest thirty-five years of earnings. One or two more years of work isn't going to change what they receive. Seniors can do the math. Many of them choose to quit working because it's just not worth it.

Some liberals in Congress have proposed that the Social Security payroll tax be raised on working people and their employers in order to expand Social Security benefits for all, regardless of their need. But unlike the income tax, everyone pays payroll tax, regardless of how little you earn. Raising a payroll tax on everyone would be a significant tax increase on millions of Americans who are barely getting by as it is. Therefore, instead of raising taxes (which seems to be the left's solution to every problem), a better approach would be to eliminate the payroll tax altogether for all Americans who have reached retirement age.

The reality of the new century is that more and more Americans will be working well past the legal retirement age. For some, like Joyce and Scott, this might be out of necessity. But for many others, including a significant percentage of my colleagues in the Senate, it will be by choice. I am now just a little over twenty years away from retirement age myself. It is hard for me to imagine retiring at sixty-five and spending the next quarter century not working. I expect to be working, doing something productive and fulfilling. I honestly know few people in my generation who do not expect the same. By the time people reach retirement age, they have already paid their fair share. We shouldn't punish them for choosing to keep working rather than immediately cashing in.

Eliminating the payroll tax on workers who have reached retirement age will do several things I dare say liberals would agree with. In addition to removing the disincentive to work, it will help seniors accelerate their savings by letting them keep more of their money. In fact, it could also make older workers more attractive to employers, since the employer's half of workers' payroll taxes would also be eliminated. Finally—and I can't believe there would be much argument about this—the elimination of the payroll tax for those past retirement age could be accomplished with little or no effect on Social Security revenues. A study cited by former deputy Social Security Commissioner Andrew Biggs found that a 10 percent increase in after-tax wages for those sixty-two and older would result in a 1.1 percent increase in the labor supply. This increase in workers, in turn, would raise federal tax revenue enough to offset about three quarters of the loss of revenue from the elimination of the payroll tax. When increased state tax revenue is taken into account, this payroll tax cut for older Americans essentially pays for itself.[9]

I have heard some people suggest that with unemployment so high and jobs so scarce, we shouldn't be pumping the labor force with more workers by giving seniors incentives to work longer. They reason that if seniors don't stop working we won't have enough jobs for younger workers. It's an interesting theory, but it's bad economics. The American economy doesn't work that way.

This argument is part of the same faulty logic used by opponents of free trade and legal immigration—and it's a cousin of the logic that says income inequality is more important than opportunity and upward mobility. All these arguments rest on two faulty assumptions. The first is that people are a liability. That more people, in our country or in our workforce, means more obligations on government. To the contrary, real conservatism views people as assets, not liabilities.

More people doesn't just mean workers or government beneficiaries. It also means more taxpayers for government and more consumers for business. So if a retiree remains in the workforce and as a result has a higher income, this means he or she will also be paying more taxes than otherwise. And the higher income also means he or she will be able to spend more at the places that employ younger Americans.

Which leads to the second false assumption: that the economy is a zero-sum game—more for you means less for me. In this case, the claim is that more jobs for older people means fewer jobs for younger people. In fact, studies show that an increase in older workers has no effect on the number of jobs for younger workers, and may even slightly boost the number of jobs for younger workers. Just like anyone else, older people who are employed have more money to spend, which creates more jobs.

More savings and more work are essential to hold off a retirement crisis. But the elephant in the living room for most Americans when they contemplate their golden years is Social Security. It can't be the only source of our income in old age, but it is the essential guarantee of a safe and secure retirement in America. It must be saved. And to be saved, it must be reformed.

Rather than reform Social Security, however, some folks in Washington would rather double down on the program as it exists and throw more money into it. Either that, or they deny there's any problem and refuse to take any action at all. When President George W. Bush offered a plan to reform the program in 2005, House Minority Leader Nancy Pelosi was asked when her Democratic colleagues would put forward their own proposal. Her answer? "Never. Is 'never' good enough for you?"[10]

Failing to modernize Social Security, however, will eventually lead to an outcome we can't buy our way out of, no matter how high we might raise taxes. The 2013 Social Security Trustees Report declared that over the next decade Social Security will pay out about $984 billion more in benefits—almost $1 trillion—than it will collect in payroll taxes. The fact is, the country has changed enormously since the passage of Social Security. Yet the basic benefit rules have failed to adjust accordingly.

Take the retirement age. In 1940, when an American turned twenty-one, his chances of living to retirement age were only about 55 to 60 percent. But today, a twenty-one-year-old's chances of reaching retirement age are around 80 percent. Since we are living longer, we are working longer. If you doubt me, I invite you to come see the United States Senate at work. There you will find plenty of evidence that more and more Americans are choosing to work well past the age of retirement.

What these longer working lives mean in practical terms is that we now have a record number of Social Security beneficiaries. And these beneficiaries, on average, are living another five to ten years longer than Social Security's earliest recipients.[11] This is good news, of course. I am blessed that my mother is still living and therefore a part of my children's lives. But it also presents us with a new dynamic we didn't have when the program was first designed.

In the past eighty years, Congress has increased the retirement age by two years, from sixty-five to sixty-seven. This is some progress in adjusting Social Security to the modern era, but not enough to ensure that the program will be there for your kids and my kids. We need to increase the retirement age for future retirees to account for the rise in life expectancy. If we act soon, we can do this without changing the retirement age for people who are currently over the age of fifty-five.

Another modernization to Social Security that should gather bipartisan support at a time when the growing divide between the rich and the poor is occupying so much political space is strengthening the program as a safety net for those at the bottom of the income scale. Americans who have worked their whole lives for low wages, like my parents, shouldn't be consigned to poverty in their old age. For these Americans, Social Security benefits are a substantial—in fact, irreplaceable—source of income in retirement.

Contrast this with high-income retirees. For wealthy retirees, monthly Social Security benefits are a less significant portion of their finances. The obvious answer is to adjust the benefits in the program to preserve and strengthen it for our children and grandchildren. Democrats resist this change on the grounds that turning Social Security into an income transfer program like traditional welfare will cause it to lose support among Americans. But this kind of ideological argument doesn't hold water. First, proposals by Democrats like Senator Elizabeth Warren to raise the amount of income subject to the payroll tax but keep benefits the same would do exactly that: turn Social Security into an income transfer payment by breaking the link between contributions and benefits. Second, it's hard to see how a program as popular as Social Security could fall out of favor with the American people by showing compassion for the less fortunate.

The demographics of Social Security have turned brutally against the program. Too few workers today support too many retirees. Increasing the benefit for all retirees would put unrealistic and unsustainable strain on the program. The answer is to reduce the growth of benefits for upper-income seniors while making the program even stronger for lower-income seniors. This wouldn't be a cut but simply a reduction in how fast the benefit will increase for wealthier retirees. Making this commonsense change will add years to Social Security's solvency. It is one of the best ways to save the program for high-income and low-income beneficiaries alike.

———

The third reform needed to avert a retirement crisis is also the most difficult: saving Medicare for all American seniors.

As with Social Security, my attachment to Medicare is deeply personal, even selfish. When my father got sick, Medicare paid for his many hospital stays. As he reached the end of his life, Medicare allowed him comfort and dignity by paying for his hospice care. My mother benefits from it to this day. Medicare, like Social Security, is absolutely essential to maintaining a secure, healthy and comfortable retirement for seniors. But Medicare, like Social Security, will cease to exist if we do nothing to reform it.

Again, this is not a scare tactic. It is simple math. In 2012 Medicare spending grew by 4.6 percent—to about $580 billion. Between now and 2022, this growth rate is expected to accelerate to around 7.4 percent per year.[12] At this rate, within eleven years the Medicare Trust Fund will run dry.

There was once a time when talking about Medicare reform was a third rail of American politics. But as we get closer to impending doom, it seems more people are at least willing to discuss serious ideas about how to save Medicare. I'm happy—even eager—to have that conversation. It needs to begin by taking a hard look at what recent reform efforts tell us about what works and what does not when it comes to making health care accessible to all Americans.

The Affordable Care Act—Obamacare—is about to turn five. The impending anniversary of the passage of this law raises the iconic question: Are you better off than you were five years ago? The answer for most Americans is an unequivocal no. Jobs have been lost. Hours have been cut. Employers have been forced to drop coverage. Premiums have skyrocketed. Millions have lost coverage they were happy with.

Obamacare has even hurt Medicare recipients by cutting about $156 billion out of Medicare Advantage. This cut was a grave miscalculation. Medicare Advantage is a shining success story that millions of seniors like my mom rely upon. In short, it allows you to receive coverage from a private provider using funding from Medicare. Its free-market structure has encouraged providers to compete for business by tacking on all sorts of value-added services for seniors. For example, one of the reasons my mom picked her current provider is because, in addition to good doctors, they pick her up and drive her to appointments.

This sort of competition in the marketplace invariably leads to two very good things: a decrease in prices and an increase in choices. Choice and competition are also at the heart of another Medicare success story: Medicare Part D. Through this market-based program, seniors have at least twenty-eight different prescription drug coverage plans to choose from, and competition has worked as a powerful cost control mechanism. The Congressional Budget Office found that total program costs are on track to be 45 percent less—or $348 billion—than initial ten-year projections.

Average monthly premiums are expected to be $31 in 2014, less than half of the $64 originally predicted. Not only does Medicare Part D's design save money, seniors love it: 95 percent of seniors enrolled in Part D find it convenient for their needs.[13]

There are important lessons in the mistakes of Obamacare and the successes of Medicare Advantage and Medicare Part D for ensuring the health and continued existence of Medicare itself. If history is any guide, the key is to avoid command-and-control rationing and instead dramatically expand health care choices for seniors. A marketplace of choices will spur competition and extend the solvency of the Medicare Trust Fund, all while making sure traditional Medicare remains an option. If we act now, we can save Medicare and provide health security to America's seniors.

The solution I support is a transition to a premium support system that would give seniors a generous but fixed amount of money with which to purchase health insurance. They could choose to buy from either Medicare or a private provider, and the choice would be theirs to make. My friend Paul Ryan is a leader when it comes to Medicare reform. During my campaign in 2010, I supported a couple of key proposals to fix the program that were detailed in his Roadmap for America's Future. Since then, he has teamed up with Oregon Democratic Senator Ron Wyden to propose a bold bipartisan plan to institute the premium support model.

The way this plan works in practice for American seniors is crucial. No one over the age of fifty-five would see a change in their benefits. For others, the government contribution they receive would be pegged to either traditional Medicare or the average bid from private providers—whichever is cheapest. This way, if seniors choose plans that cost more than that benchmark, they would have to pay the difference. If they choose cheaper plans, they would get to keep the savings. The level of support would increase with age, and poor seniors and those with the most health care needs would get more support.

The way this plan works to save Medicare is also crucial. Competition between private plans and traditional fee-for-service Medicare will create choices for seniors while controlling costs for taxpayers. Some providers will offer the same health benefits as traditional Medicare but for less money. Others will offer innovative benefits that are specifically focused around the needs of seniors. The CBO predicts that by 2030 Medicare spending under a premium support plan would be 7 percent less per person than under the current system.[14]

As I mentioned, this reform will not be easy—worthwhile endeavors rarely are. But anyone who considers Medicare worth saving will give this plan a serious look. And any American who cares about the security of his or her retirement will demand leaders who do.

———

In a few months, I will turn forty-four years old. It seems like just a few days ago that I was graduating high school, or standing at the altar, or welcoming our first child home. The older I get, the more I am reminded of how quickly things move, and how it's never too early to start planning ahead for the next phase of life. As a citizen and a husband, this means saving for retirement. It means seeing what it will take to be ready when the time comes. It also means preparing for the fact that, if nothing changes, by the time I reach full retirement age at sixty-seven, Social Security and Medicare will have been insolvent for years.

I have an additional responsibility, though: the responsibility that belongs to all who are elected to serve. My responsibility—to the American people, to my parents, to myself—is to save these programs. But many of my colleagues in Washington—especially big-government liberals—don't seem to feel the same way. As a senator, then as a candidate and now as president, Barack Obama has never offered a serious proposal to fix Medicare and Social Security. The same goes for Hillary Clinton. Instead, they consistently have chosen to use any proposals to save these programs as political weapons against Republicans. As they do, it becomes increasingly clear that big-government liberals are more interested in winning elections than saving these programs.

It may help a politician defeat an opponent at the ballot box, but the ultimate price of inaction will be paid by future retirees. What many in politics seem to have forgotten is that we are here to serve the public interest, not posture politically. Yet so many politicians are unable—or unwilling—to acknowledge that their lack of action dooms the very programs they claim they are committed to preserving.

Partisan politics in America has always been contentious. But throughout our history, on issues of generational importance, our leaders have agreed to put aside politics for the sake of our people. If ever there was an issue worthy of this solidarity, it is preserving a secure retirement for twenty-first-century seniors. Should we fail to address it, history will point its finger at all who stood aside or stood in the way.

The next president of the United States will be unable to serve two full terms without confronting this looming crisis. The sooner we act, the less disruptive these reforms will be. In these pages I have presented an agenda for addressing this crisis head-on. I'm ready to take whatever political fallout it generates. But most important, I am eager to work with anyone—Republican or Democrat—who will work in good faith on these reforms.

Chapter Seven

VALUES—AND THE FAMILIES THAT TEACH THEM

India is a young woman with an American success story for our times. She rose from poverty and homelessness and beat the odds, not just because she overcame a lack of *things* in her life. No, she's special because she overcame a lack of *values* in her home— the values transmitted by strong families and stable communities. India's story is remarkable and inspirational. But it's also the exception that proves the rules about what it takes to achieve the American Dream.

Today India is a graduate of the University of Florida with a master's degree and a career as a school administrator. But she was born with the odds stacked against her. She grew up in public housing in Venice, Florida, the ninth of ten children to a mother struggling with alcohol and a father who was haphazardly in and out of their lives. She talks matter-of-factly about the abuse she suffered at home and the conditions in her neighborhood. Loud music blaring all night. Drugs sold openly on the corner. Alcohol everywhere—inside and outside her home. She recalls being beaten with extension cords until she was covered with welts. She was often reluctant to tell the police when her mother hit her because she had to be home to care for her mentally handicapped little sister. Still, the police were at India's home so often that by the time she was fifteen the cops knew her by name.

As bad as things were, India says, it was in eleventh grade when things "really started to fall apart." It was Christmas Eve, and India had finished her shift at the Publix supermarket and returned home. When she knocked on the door to their apartment, her mother didn't answer.

"I was knocking on the door, knocking on the door. Tears rolling down my eyes," she says. "I eventually realized around twelve o'clock in the morning that she was not letting me in. I was kicked out. I was homeless."

This began a period in which India spent her days wandering the streets and staying with friends at night. Her goal, she says, was to do what she had to do to be able to go to school in the morning. School was her refuge from the chaos in her life. She didn't tell her teachers she was homeless, but still she managed to attend classes—and not just any classes, but difficult classes, such as precalculus and honors English. Somehow, despite the shambles of her life outside the school walls, inside them she found enrichment and stability, even excellence.

India challenges us to think about what matters in preparing children for happy, successful lives. I have always felt that I had a privileged childhood. Not because we had a lot of material things or knew a lot of important people—we didn't. But I was rich in the things that matter. I had a strong, stable home, a place where I was loved. I had parents and grandparents in my life who encouraged me to dream big, and who supported me as I pursued those dreams.

India had none of these things. There was no encouragement in her home to go to school and succeed—quite the opposite. Presented with India's report card full of A's, her mother typically responded by staring at her without emotion and then telling India to "clean my house." Worse yet, there was none of the unconditional love a child needs to have confidence that she has a future and a purpose on the planet. India tells a heartbreaking story about one day when she was homeless, talking to the police about finding a place to stay. As they were talking, her father happened to ride by on a bicycle. She remembers telling the police officers eagerly, "That's my dad! He'll take me in. Ask him." So the police told India's father that she needed a place to stay. He looked at her, then at the police officers, and said the words India has never forgotten: "She's not my daughter. Do what you want with her." And then he left.

To hear India's childhood stories and to see the successful, confident woman she has become is to ask, *How?* How could a girl with so many strikes against her rise to achieve her dreams when so many others can't? Social scientists are in virtually unanimous agreement that, considering the odds, India shouldn't have succeeded in climbing out of poverty. Children like her—raised in poverty by single parents—get in more trouble with the law and perform more poorly in school than kids of two married parents. They are less likely to finish high school, let alone college, and are more apt to get pregnant young. In short, the children of single parents are more likely to be born poor and they are more likely to stay poor—four to five times more likely than children raised by married parents.[1]

In truth, we've known for some time the disadvantages suffered by children in single-parent homes. What is less appreciated—but more relevant today than ever—is how the decline of the family has affected social and economic mobility in America. That is, how the rise of broken, single-parent families has affected the American Dream. Few people in Washington like to talk about it, but the decline of the family is a major factor limiting the ability of many Americans to get ahead. Isabel Sawhill of the left-leaning Brookings Institution reports that of the children born to low-income women, the children born to never married mothers are *three times* more likely to stay poor than children born to continuously married mothers.[2]

A landmark study that looked exclusively at the ability of Americans to move up the economic ladder in different communities found that the strongest influence on upward mobility is family structure. More than racial segregation, more than education, more than inequality, the number of single parents in a community is most determinative of upward mobility. The study found that in a city like Salt Lake City, with low numbers of single parents, children in the poorest families have an 11 percent chance of making it to the top level of income. In a city like Atlanta, with high numbers of single parents, they have only a 4.4 percent chance of making it.[3]

So why aren't all the politicians and reporters who claim to be

concerned with the gap between the rich and the poor concentrat-
ing on the family? One reason is that the left spends a lot of time
and resources creating government *substitutes* for the family. But if
the state could simply step in and fill the role of two committed,
caring parents, then India's story wouldn't be so special. The poor
in America have plenty of government interventions in their lives.
What they too often lack is something government simply cannot
provide: a source of unconditional love that transmits the values of
hard work, self-control and self-esteem. No one is born with these
values, yet in order to find real success—truly rewarding and
happy lives—people need them just as much as they need an education and a job.

India, too, has had plenty of government involvement in her
life, from welfare to food stamps to government literally putting a
roof over her head after her mother kicked her out. But the thing
that made the difference—the reason we are able to celebrate her
story today—is that she found a source of love and direction. Ask
India why she was able to rise above homelessness, an abusive
mother and an absent father, and she cites two things: her faith in
God, and a mentor—a red-haired, blue-eyed woman who came to
regard India, an African American, as her daughter.

When she was in seventh grade—still doing well in school but
starting to act out and develop an angry, bad attitude—India met
the woman who would change her life through a program called
Take Stock in Children. The program targets poor middle school–
aged kids and gets them thinking about their futures. It provides
ninth graders with a scholarship for higher education, but, more
important in India's case, it sets them up with a mentor. It was her

mentor, Sharon, who gave India the love and guidance that more fortunate children get from their parents.

Sharon literally made a better future a possibility for India. She would drive her around Venice to a nice area of town, point to a big, expensive house and say, "India, someone owns that. You could do that one day. Couldn't you see yourself in a house like that?" No one in India's family had ever gone to college. Sharon was the first to introduce the possibility to India. "It was a completely foreign idea to me," India says. "But she put hope in me. She never let me feel sorry for myself and she never let me feel like I was incompetent or I couldn't succeed."

So India poured herself into school because she knew it would please her mentor. When the other kids at school teased her and accused her of acting "white" because she studied and read books by Laura Ingalls Wilder, India found the strength inside herself and from her mentor to ignore them. She found a peer group who shared her ambitions and she emulated them. And when India eventually went to the University of Florida on a full-ride scholarship from the Gates Foundation—she literally went overnight from a homeless shelter in Sarasota to a dorm room—it was her mentor's house she went to for Christmas and spring break.

"In spite of my failures, my downfalls and my weaknesses, she still loves me," India says of Sharon. "She's shown me love even when I've made mistakes. She's shown me love."

Through the grace of God and the generosity of people like Sharon, India is achieving her American Dream. I was a supporter of Take Stock in Children in the Florida legislature and I continue to support programs that help lift disadvantaged kids. But the void they are being asked to fill is huge, and growing. The problem of children being born without two married parents is no longer confined to an underclass of Americans. A significant portion of the American middle class is now teetering on the brink of the cultural chasm of single parenthood.

More important than the demographics of this problem is its moral urgency. We can no longer plead ignorance to the effects of single parenthood in the lives of children. Many single mothers are heroic in their efforts to provide for their children, and many succeed. But our responsibility is to prevent women and children from being forced to struggle alone in the first place—and we know what it takes to do that. It is now unacceptable—if it ever was otherwise—for a politician who claims to care about income inequality to ignore the plight of the American family. And it is unacceptable—and it was ever so—to attempt to shout down those who express concern about the family with charges of racism and sexism. The children of single parents start life disadvantaged and the overwhelming majority of them never catch up. They are the face of the decline of the American Dream.

One statistic rarely captures the dimensions of a major social, cultural and economic crisis as well as this one: the average age of an American woman's first marriage is now higher than the average age of her first birth. Unwed childbearing, in other words, is the new normal. Of the roughly 450 births that have occurred in America in the last hour, 180 of them were to unwed mothers.

Having children outside marriage has grown among all kinds

of Americans, but it has not grown equally. For the most educated, the percentage of births to never married women is still small, just 6 percent, compared with 2 percent in 1982. For the least educated, the rate has grown to 54 percent from 33 percent. But the greatest increase has been among the moderately educated—high school graduates with some college education but no degree. Not coincidentally, these are the Americans who are struggling most in the new economy. For them, the percentage of children being born outside of marriage has climbed from 13 percent in 1982 to an astounding 44 percent today.[4]

Brad Wilcox of the University of Virginia describes the group of mostly working-class Americans who are experiencing an explosion in out-of-wedlock births as being at a tipping point: Either they can continue to have more and more children out of wedlock and dim their prospects for success, or they can hang on to the institution of the family and begin to reverse the declines they've suffered.[5] Which direction they choose—and it is, still, a choice—will be a critical moment in the history of the American family. Single parenthood—with all its attendant poverty and chaos—tends to replicate itself through the generations. The daughters of single parents have higher rates of early pregnancy themselves, trapping their children in the same seemingly never-ending cycle of poverty that they themselves are caught in. Once lost to generational poverty, these Americans will be difficult to bring back. And the data are telling us that time is not on our side. Younger Americans are growing less and less attached to the institution of marriage. While the rate of unwed childbirth is around 40 percent for all women, for the members of the millennial generation, those now eighteen to thirty-three years old, 47 percent of births are outside marriage. Today, an astounding one third of our children live apart from their fathers. One in three.[6]

It's not an exaggeration to say that the breakdown of the family is the single greatest challenge facing America. The question is, what can be done about it? As Ronald Reagan used to say, there are no easy answers, but there are simple ones. The first step is pretty basic and surprisingly controversial: just admitting we have a problem.

In his 2014 State of the Union speech, President Obama dedicated his remarks to combating income inequality and immobility. He went on to talk about many things—taxes, trade, job training, global warming, the minimum wage. He even brought up my name when he talked about the Earned Income Tax Credit. But never once did he mention the health of the American family. He and his liberal colleagues have declared income inequality the defining challenge of our time, but they have had little to say about what might be its greatest cause. This is a man—himself the child of a single mother—with a unique ability to reach the poor and minority communities most affected by the breakdown of the family. That he has chosen not to address this crisis is a tragically wasted opportunity.

Truth be told, no one in Washington has been very effective in addressing the crisis of marriage and the family. On the right, there are many voices raised in promotion and defense of two-parent families. But these advocates have often been portrayed, for reasons both fair and unfair, as judgmental and moralistic. The left has been worse. When those on the left have been forced to acknowledge the problem, they've tended to either deny that there is anything that can be done about it or to insist that poverty is driving the breakdown of the family rather than the other way around. But America has gone through tough economic times before without also seeing our families destroyed. The Great Depression, for instance, didn't result in families breaking apart at the rate they have been in the past four decades.

The fact is that the cultural and economic forces behind the decline in marriage and the two-parent family are complex. There is little doubt, for instance, that the decline of work among young men is a factor in declining marriage rates. For young mothers, men who are broke and out of work—despite the fact that they are the fathers of their children—are less attractive marriage prospects. Policies that encourage work, such as the Wage Enhancement Credit I described in Chapter Three, will allow these young men to better provide for a family. But to argue that poverty is the only thing driving the decline in marriage is to engage in deep denial. It is to deny the incentives built into government programs that discourage marriage among the poor. It is to deny the powerful pull of a culture that regards unwed childbearing as nothing more or less than a lifestyle choice—and vilifies those who would criticize it as perpetrators of a "war on women." It is also to deny millennia of human history and hundreds of years of American history that put the family at the center of human progress. Throughout our nation's history, when families and the values they teach have flourished, so has our culture—and our economy.

The first step in restoring the American Dream for American families, then, is to simply recognize the link between strong families and a strong America. If we are willing to say that smoking causes cancer or that childhood obesity leads to serious health risks later in life, then we must also be willing to acknowledge that broken families cause poverty and diminished futures for our children.

Second, we must recognize that bad government policies are a contributing factor in the decline of families and the values they teach. Instead of fortifying our people through pro-family policy making, government has done the opposite. Consider the case of Darnell and Charlotte, a couple in Baltimore.

Darnell and Charlotte thought they were doing it right. Six months after they met, they married. A few months later, Charlotte was pregnant with their first child. She had been supporting a daughter from a previous relationship, along with a young cousin, with the $824 she made each month by working three jobs, plus food stamps and welfare benefits. But when she married Darnell, his additional income from a construction job made their family income too high to continue to receive government assistance. So when the new baby came, Charlotte failed to disclose that she was married to Darnell on her application for assistance for her new baby. She also had to report Darnell to another state agency as the father of her child in order to receive other assistance, which alerted the state that he owed child support for a daughter from a previous relationship. The rules are there for good reasons—to keep people from gaming the system and to make fathers support their children—but the net effect was to penalize Darnell and Charlotte from doing the right thing—getting married.

Incentives matter. Earlier, in Chapter Three, I talked about the way our existing poverty programs discourage moving from government assistance to work and independence by leveling an extremely high tax—in the form of decreased benefits—on the poor as they begin to work and earn more money. The example of Darnell and Charlotte shows that the same disincentives to work that are built into our government assistance programs are also a disincentive to marry.

These government-created disincentives to marriage affect the dependent poor and the working poor alike. In testimony before Congress in 2014, Robert Doar, who oversaw welfare reform for New York City, talked about the perverse incentives against marriage in the Earned Income Tax Credit, the refundable tax credit designed to boost the incomes of the working poor. A single parent of two children who earns $15,000 a year receives an EITC benefit of around $4,100. But if she marries, her benefit decreases by over twenty cents for every dollar the family earns above $15,040. So if she marries a man who earns just $10,000 a year, her EITC benefit drops by almost 50 percent, from over $4,000 to just over $2,000.[7]

The same kind of work and marriage tax is embedded in our other poverty programs. That's why I have proposed reforms that would build on the success of the EITC in encouraging work among the poor. My federal Wage Enhancement Credit, explained at length in Chapter Three, would give workers making less than $20,000 a year a 30 percent credit, making a job that might not make ends meet on its own a realistic alternative to welfare. A critical difference with the current EITC is that the Wage Enhancement Credit would be directed at the individual, regardless of family size. This means that a couple like Charlotte and Darnell wouldn't lose benefits when they combine their income in marriage. My proposal would also encourage marriage by encouraging work among young men, making them better prospects as husbands and fathers to their children.

The Wage Enhancement Credit would work hand in hand with a consolidation of federal poverty programs into a Flex Fund, which would give the states the freedom and flexibility to create programs to encourage work and marriage. The city of Baltimore, home to Charlotte and Darnell, is conducting such an experiment. Officials there have recognized that current public assistance programs were designed in another era, when most children ended up in homes with single moms because of divorce—thus leading to the emphasis on replacing or recovering the income lost with the husband. Today's couples are more likely to cohabitate and have children from previous relationships. Marriage remains a goal for many of them. So public officials are experimenting with ways to help couples stay together through job training, parent and financial counseling, and helping men like Darnell meet their obligations to their children without jeopardizing their relationships with their current partners and their ability to support new children.[8]

As we've seen, though, single-parent families aren't just a problem among the poor and government dependent. Unwed births are increasing—and marriage is declining—most rapidly among the high school–educated lower middle class. Our current tax code roundly penalizes marriage by hitting married couples with taxes that two otherwise identical singles would be spared from. Senator Mike Lee's and my pro-family tax plan will end the marriage penalty by doubling the tax threshold for joint filers. And it will make parents more financially stable by the addition of our new $2,500 per child tax credit and making it deductible, meaning whatever isn't saved through a reduction of a couple's income and payroll tax liability would be received in cash.

Finally, the institution of marriage itself is in need of defense today. Marriage is one of those things that, like having a child, is almost universally experienced but very personally lived. Government can play a role, but ultimately the decision to marry is a very personal one. And so it is that stopping the decline of marriage must begin on that personal level, by continuing to advocate for our values in the public square and by raising our children to perpetuate them in their own lives.

In our contemporary discussions on marriage, we must also acknowledge the national debate regarding the very definition of marriage. On this point, I—along with millions of my fellow Americans—firmly believe that marriage is a unique societal institution so important to the formation of strong and successful people that we have traditionally defined it and enshrined it in our laws as the union of one man and one woman.

We have done so because thousands of years of human history have taught us that the ideal setting for children to grow up in is with a mother and a father committed to each other, living together and sharing the responsibility of raising their children.

It is for this reason and this reason alone that I continue to believe marriage should be defined as one man and one woman. It is neither my place nor my intention to dictate to anyone who they are allowed to love or live with.

The question is not whether we should discriminate against anyone on the basis of his or her sexuality. We should not. The question is how our laws should define the union of two people in a marriage. And because I believe the marriage of one man and one woman is so important to a strong society, I believe that it should hold a special status in our laws. At a time when the American family is threatened as never before, redefining it away from the union of one man and one woman only promises to weaken it as a child-rearing, values-conveying institution.

My view on this places me opposite the views of a growing number of Americans. And as attitudes change, we have seen state laws change the definition of marriage as well. I do not agree with or support these changes. But I also do not question that the elected representatives in the individual states have the right to make these changes.

The trend that I will not accept, however, is the growing attitude that belief in traditional marriage equates to bigotry and hatred. Just as California has a right to redefine marriage to include same-sex couples, Florida has a right to define it as one man and one woman.

Furthermore, while I oppose redefining marriage, I also oppose discrimination, harassment and violence against anyone because of his or her sexual identity. It is possible to believe that marriage should remain the union of one man and one woman while also condemning violence or abusive behavior toward gay people, or those instances around the world of nations attempting to criminalize homosexuality.

Some activists will not accept this, of course. They seek to have gay marriage serve as a litmus test for how we view or treat gay people. As of late, they have sought to punish and ostracize those who do not agree with them. But tolerance is a two-way street. Those who advocate for gay marriage should not allow their passion to blind them to the fact that they must share our nation and its challenges with what remains a sizable percentage of Americans who continue to support traditional marriage. Just as we must respect their right to advocate for changes in our marriage laws, they must also recognize our right to stand up for our own views.

Of all the topics I have addressed in this book, the preservation of the American family is by far the most difficult. This is complex, fraught territory for any public official. But it is no longer acceptable to throw up our collective hands and run away from the issue. We know now that the stakes are too high for any more polite averting our eyes to the state of the American family. Paying lip service will no longer suffice. Real lives and real futures are at stake. The health of our economy, our exceptionalism as a nation, the very *survival* of the American Dream is caught up with the survival of the American family. Using the family as a political wedge issue—by the right or by the left—must be called out as the dangerous opportunism that it is.

And here, the responsibility—and the hypocrisy—does not lie

with all Americans equally. As we've seen, less-educated, lower-income Americans are experiencing an epidemic of broken marriages and single-parent families. Meanwhile, those at the top levels of income and education in our society are clinging to—and in many cases rediscovering—more traditional values. Less than 5 percent of college-educated white women have children outside of marriage, for example, compared with around 40 percent of white women with just a high school degree. And after growing in frequency during the 1970s and mid-1980s, divorce is now also a rarity among the upper classes.

American elites, in short, practice the old-fashioned values of work, thrift, marriage before children and delayed gratification. But in the words of American Enterprise Institute author Charles Murray, they don't "preach what they practice." Liberal elites in Washington, New York and Hollywood too often have standards for their children at home that they refuse to advocate for other people's children when they're making laws, movies, television and magazines. Television executives in Hollywood and software designers in Silicon Valley who wouldn't consider having a child outside of marriage regularly produce popular entertainment that celebrates precisely that. Even many Washington policy makers who are in church every Sunday refuse to advocate for traditional faith values for fear of committing the cardinal sin of today's liberalism: being "judgmental."

But America has been "judgmental" before—and to good effect. Our elites have even helped. Time and again, we've reached a judgment as a nation that certain behaviors are harmful and should no longer be tolerated. We've mounted campaigns involving lawmakers, business and the entertainment industry to send strong societal messages. The campaigns against smoking, drunk driving and childhood obesity come to mind. We haven't eliminated these problems altogether, but we've changed hearts and minds and we've done so by embracing—rather than avoiding—being judgmental.

Even on delicate issues like teenage sex and pregnancy, despite the general resistance of many at the commanding heights of our culture to "preach what they practice," we've been able to send the message that this activity is no longer acceptable. Teen pregnancy, birth and abortion rates are at historic lows. There are a number of reasons for this. One of the most interesting I've heard is that shows like MTV's *16 and Pregnant* have persuaded young viewers to put off sex and childbearing. One study of viewers of the show, which follows teenagers dealing with the sleepless nights and loss of freedom that come with having a baby, showed that the rate of teenage pregnancy declined faster in areas where teenagers watched more MTV programming, including *16 and Pregnant*.[9]

Marriage and family are bigger and more profound issues than even teen pregnancy. Still, with the support of transformed government programs, a national campaign bringing together the entertainment industry, civic groups, churches and elected officials could begin to change American hearts and minds on the issue of marriage. Reminding our fellow citizens of the values that we've always embraced as a nation—the values the most successful Americans cling to today—could begin to turn the tide on the decline of marriage. It's not a magic bullet. American families still suffer from a lack of job opportunities and a lack of skills for the new economy, not to mention soaring health care, college and housing costs. But the very real cultural issues that are contributing to the decline of marriage—the easy acceptance of unwed motherhood and absent fathers, the "just do it if it feels good" ethos—these are susceptible to some good old-fashioned moral judgment.

Such a campaign, of course, requires leadership, and what we have in Washington today on issues of marriage and the family is the opposite of leadership. Instead of offering America's struggling single moms and dads help in transcending their situations, Democrats employ the deeply cynical "war on women" strategy to keep them—and their votes—just where they are. Despite the clear, uncontested evidence that single parenthood creates significant challenges for children, for mothers and even for fathers, any mention of efforts to address it is greeted as more of the conservative "animus toward women." But who is it, really, that has the best interests of single women and American families at heart? Those who fixate on a fictional "war on women"? Or those who are eager to reform our poverty programs, our tax code and our moral sensibility to support work and family?

I'm not blind to the work we have to do to convince women struggling to raise families alone of the rightness of our cause. But when I think of a young woman like India, I know that the ideas and the policies I have discussed in this book are a natural fit for a young American of ambition and determination like her. I have no idea how she votes or what her politics are. I know only that these policies focus on bringing opportunity within reach of everyone. We must never forget that by confronting our family crisis, we are also confronting the idea that gave birth to our country: the idea that everyone deserves the chance to go as far as their dreams, work and talent will take them.

It is this belief that has turned America into the single most generous and caring nation on the planet. Each generation in our history has instilled in the next a deep sense of duty toward those who are struggling. In our families, in our homes, in the examples of our parents, we have learned not to sit back and wait for government to step in to help those in need, but to take it upon ourselves.

This value should be reflected in our government too, through policies that empower our people to achieve their true potential. People are always grateful for financial assistance, but after that, they want the ability to achieve true independence. This means they need the education that will lead to employable skills, the economic growth that will lead to a good job—and, yes, the values that will lead to successful and fulfilling lives.

We can cut taxes, reduce regulations, improve higher education and spark economic growth, but if we do not address the challenges facing American families, millions will continue to be denied an equal opportunity to achieve a better life. Solving all the other challenges facing America—from joblessness to poverty to inequality—is contingent upon solving this one.

So when our children and their children look back decades from now, let it be said that we did what was necessary to preserve what made us special. Let it be said that we reclaimed the values of a strong people, and in doing so preserved the legacy of the greatest nation in the history of the world.

Afterword

Since I began writing this book in the spring of 2014, Americans have witnessed a time of extraordinary upheaval around the world, and unprecedented distrust in government here at home.

When I began writing, most Americans had never heard of ISIL. Since then, we have witnessed the murder of our own journalists, the savage enslavement of women and girls, and an expanding arc of death and destruction across the Middle East. The terrorists President Obama once dismissed as the "JV squad" now control vast swaths of Iraq and Syria. And when I began writing, few would have guessed that Russia would upend decades of regional balance and challenge European security. Nonetheless, Russia invaded Ukraine and hundreds of innocent travelers were murdered when a Malaysian passenger plane was shot from the sky.

The list goes on. A modern-day plague erupted and has raged through West Africa, eventually reaching America's shores. Innocent Syrians are slaughtered at the whim of a tyrant. Hamas rains terror down on Israel. China continues its provocations in the South China Sea. Peaceful protestors in Venezuela are met with violence from their own government—and then a corrupt United Nations elects that government to its most august body.

Americans once trusted our institutions to protect us from the dangers of the world and to champion our interests in our daily lives. In the institutions of the presidency and the Congress we placed our trust to lead our nation abroad in pursuit of our interests and highest ideals. This trust was not misplaced. Providing for the common defense is the highest responsibility of our elected leaders. The Constitution assigns seventeen separate duties to Congress, six of which deal exclusively with national defense—more than any other area. And as the chief executive and commander in chief, the president has a unique role in our national defense, one that only he or she can play: to have the foresight to see threats developing and to lead the American people in dealing with these threats.

National defense is the first and highest calling of government. And all of the threats to the American Dream discussed in this book—from the decline of good jobs to the need for education reform to prepare Americans for the jobs of the twenty-first century—are tied, either directly or indirectly, to our ability to protect our interests around the globe. Our economic prosperity—and with it our jobs—depends on our ability to sell products and services to other nations, to communicate openly and reliably, and to travel freely. Millions of our best jobs today and in the future depend on foreign trade.

Still, debates about the proper strength of our military and the proper application of our strength around the world—whether to get involved in foreign lands or not—are as old as the republic. There have always been those who argue that America shouldn't concern herself with the affairs of the world—that what happens an ocean away bears little relevance to our people. Some of these men were members of the first Congress. When their president, George Washington, delivered the first ever State of the Union address, he asserted the need for American strength in order to protect the new republic. Washington said, "To prepare for war is one of the most effectual means of preserving the peace." But Congress disagreed. They assumed our hard-won independence meant the threats of the Old World had finally become irrelevant. They believed the nation could now afford to devote itself exclusively to domestic issues. So, against Washington's wishes, they cut the navy's funding. Our ships were taken out of service, our sailors sent home.

But even then, America's economy relied heavily on trade with Europe. And without a navy to protect them, our merchant ships were easy prey for marauding, extortionist bands of North African pirates known as the Barbary pirates. Throughout the Mediterranean, they attacked, killed and enslaved our sailors. They seized ships and their cargo and demanded exorbitant ransoms. But there was nothing we could do. America was defenseless. Even after we recommissioned our navy and sent it across the Atlantic to battle the pirates, it took nearly fifteen years and two Barbary Wars to secure the safe passage of our ships and the continuation of trade with Europe.

From the Barbary pirates America learned—or should have learned—an important lesson: We must be prepared for threats wherever they arise, because our nation is never isolated from the world. Even then, at a time when our connections to the world were limited to a slow procession of merchant ships, tremors in global affairs could fracture the foundations of our domestic economy. This is true today as never before. Americans can now connect with the world from their living rooms with a smartphone or an iPad—no ship or even airplane is necessary. The same is true for entrepreneurs, artists—and terrorists—in other countries. What happens across the planet can have a greater impact on your family than what happens down the street.

Americans are rightly and understandably preoccupied with simply making ends meet these days—paying down that loan or holding on to the house. It's the job of our leaders to keep their eye on the outside threats that make doing these mundane things harder—or might prevent us from doing them at all. Unfortunately, too many leaders in both parties, including our president and some who aspire to be president, have shown they would rather wait for poll numbers to change than demonstrate the leadership necessary to shape public opinion.

Once again, America finds itself with some leaders who believe we can ignore the world without consequences here at home. Apparently they're oblivious to the reality that we are less insulated from global events than ever.

Instead of doing the hard work of outlining the costs of weakness and inaction to the American people, they have taken the political path of least resistance. Our leaders have advocated leaving our allies to fend for themselves. They have proposed and enacted massive reductions in defense spending. They have tried to convince Americans the world would be fine without our leadership. Worse, they have told us that America would be fine regardless of the chaos that erupts in a leaderless world.

No single president, no single party and no single Congress has been solely at fault. But a striking shift has occurred at the hands of our current president. In sharp contrast to the "peace through strength" leadership of George Washington and Ronald Reagan, the president has made *reducing* American strength and engagement an active priority. When he delivered his first inaugural address, instead of reassuring our allies, he spoke directly to our enemies, indicating willingness—even eagerness—to change our nation's approach to them. He said, "We will extend a hand if you are willing to unclench your fist." But the president didn't wait for our enemies to take a less aggressive stance against America—to unclench their fists—before he extended his hand to them. Even as they continued to threaten, target and even kill Americans, this administration went to work stripping parts from the engine of American strength. Defense spending has been cut dramatically and disproportionately—by 21 percent since 2010 when adjusted for inflation. The army is set to be reduced to pre–World War II levels. The navy is at pre–World War I levels. The air force has the smallest and oldest combat force in its history.

To the world, this decline in American strength has sent a message to both our friends and our enemies. Our friends doubt our resolve and hesitate to join us in combating threats. And our adversaries are emboldened by what they perceive as our diminished military presence. For proof, recall the way Russian dictator Vladimir Putin scoffed at the president's modest attempts to impose sanctions during the Ukraine crisis. Or recall how the Syrian tyrant Bashar al-Assad declined to take America's threats seriously, used chemical weapons on his own people and still remains in power.

Here at home, the president's foreign policy retreat and ensuing global chaos has undermined the American people's faith, not just in the institutions of government to keep us safe, but in the very promise and power of the American ideal. The pride we once took in our global leadership has withered into uncertainty. The hope that America could fix international crises has turned to hope that we will stop making them worse.

For me—and I hope the vast majority of my colleagues in Congress—the ongoing discussion about the nature and extent of America's role in the world isn't just an academic discussion. I am keenly aware that my decisions impact each and every American, sometimes in personal and profound ways. Over the last fourteen years, thousands of Americans have lost mothers, fathers, sons and daughters as part of our effort to defeat terrorism and bring freedom to Iraq and Afghanistan. These sacrifices have left many Americans understandably weary. Many of us are also discouraged by the nature of disputes in the world, particularly the Middle East, which seems to pit one bad actor against another. We're tired that our efforts are so often unappreciated. And we wonder, with all the problems here at home, why we should spend our money and effort abroad.

There is no denying that a globally engaged America comes at a steep price. But the history of our young nation shows that a lack of American engagement in global leadership exacts an even higher price. Imagine for a moment the kind of world we would live in if America had sat out the twentieth century. Imagine if the beaches of Normandy had never been touched by American boots, if American aid hadn't helped alleviate the AIDS crisis in Africa or if nuclear proliferation had continued unfettered by U.S. leadership. It's no exaggeration to say that the world would be less prosperous—even that the majority of democracies would fail to exist—had America failed to lead.

When we have listened to the voices urging us to retreat from the world, we have failed to meet the threats growing abroad until it was almost too late. In November 2013 I stood at a podium at the American Enterprise Institute in Washington D.C. and warned that we were on the verge of repeating that mistake once again. Other nations were not sitting idly by waiting for America to, as President Obama put it, "nation-build at home." Tragically, events of the past year have borne out this warning. From Libya to Syria to Egypt to Ukraine, this administration simply shrugs as threats fester. When it does act, it fails to communicate any consistent rationale for military use.

We can't change the past, but we can begin to build a foundation for future American strength and leadership. At a minimum, the events of the past year have made it clear what a twenty-first-century American foreign policy should *not* look like. It should not be tentative about—or even hostile to—American leadership. It should not be poll driven. And it should not seek to deny the simple truth that the world is at its safest when America is at its strongest.

Rebuilding American strength and restoring trust in our national security institutions rests on achieving three objectives. First, we must recognize that, in a globalized world, conflict breeds economic disruption. If a band of pirates was able to wreak havoc on our economy in the late eighteenth century, then ISIL, a nuclear Iran, an aggressive China or a resurgent Russia can certainly do so in the twenty-first. We must boldly oppose efforts by other nations to infringe upon the freedom of international waters, airspace, cyberspace and outer space.

Second, we need to have moral clarity regarding what we stand for and why. This means being unabashed in support of the spread of economic and political freedom. It means reinforcing our alliances based on these principles. And it means resisting efforts by rising and resurgent powers to subjugate their neighbors.

Finally, we need American strength. America under this president has simply not been at its strongest. Waiting for our adversaries to unclench their fists so we can shake their hands has not proven a responsible or effective strategy. The "don't do stupid stuff" approach has proven self-contradictory. We must instead demonstrate a strength in defense capabilities that, as Presidents Washington and Reagan envisioned, leaves our enemies unwilling to provoke us. Yet times have changed since Reagan's historic buildup. A strong national defense in the twenty-first century will require a defense agenda built for the twenty-first century—one that ensures the superiority of our technological advances, armed forces and intelligence capabilities.

Rebuilding American strength for the twenty-first century begins with a willingness to allocate an appropriate amount of money toward our defense needs. There is no denying that the fiscal challenges facing our nation are daunting. In fact, I believe one of the greatest risks to our national security is our federal debt. But it's important to remember that defense spending is not the primary driver of our debt. Defense makes up only about 16 percent of the federal budget—and that amount is declining. It is Social Security and Medicare that comprise a staggering 37 percent of the federal budget—and that amount is rising. This is why I've proposed ways to reform these important entitlement programs to make them sustainable.

In 2011, then Secretary of Defense Robert Gates proposed a defense budget for 2012 that was forward-thinking, strategy-driven and also fiscally sustainable. The bipartisan National Defense Panel also recommends that we move to fulfill the Gates budget goals as soon as possible. As it is, our defense budget is running about $1 trillion short of this bipartisan funding goal.

Basing our defense budgets on strategy and not math, as Secretary Gates has proposed, will allow us both to modernize our military to make sure it is on the cutting edge today and to innovate to make sure we remain there tomorrow. As it is, far from modernizing and innovating within our military force, we are actually going backward in the area of force levels. This may have gone largely unnoticed in the United States, but it sure hasn't among our adversaries. China, in particular, is sprinting up behind us, rapidly closing the gap in readiness and strength, and now America must run faster than ever just to maintain our current level of superiority. For the first time ever, we are reacting to China's advances in capabilities rather than having China react to ours.

Along with this loss of faith in our government's ability to ensure the national defense is a devastating—but deserved—distrust in the capacity and competence of government to ensure our domestic tranquillity. Americans' trust in our institutions has been waning for decades, but the past year or so has been a particularly painful reckoning. A truly mind-boggling list of failures and betrayals covers virtually every part of government—the disastrous rollout and subsequent failure of Obamacare, the targeting of conservative groups by the IRS, the broken promise to our veterans by a dysfunctional Veterans Affairs, the State Department cover-up of Benghazi, the Secret Service's failure to adequately protect the president, the incompetence of our public health system in the initial stages of the Ebola crisis . . . All of these lapses have brought Americans' trust in government to all-time lows. The fact that these failures were so often accompanied by dogmatic assertions to the contrary by government officials has only deepened this distrust.

I began writing this book knowing that the American Dream is threatened by the extreme stresses our schools, our businesses and even our families face today. As I write these words almost a year later, it is more clear than ever that the governmental institutions that are supposed to help Americans succeed—to help educate our kids, ensure a fair playing field for businesses and support American families—are less capable and less trusted than at any time in our nation's history. Part of the reason is a lack of leadership in Washington. But a related and more significant reason—

the one that I've attempted to address with a reform agenda outlined in these pages—is that our institutions are outdated and outmoded. They represent a twentieth-century big-government command-and-control approach that, if it was ever successful, is destined to fail in a globalized, technology-driven, twenty-first-century America. We simply can't solve today's problems with yesterday's answers.

When I became speaker of the Florida House of Representatives in 2007, I gave a speech laying out a plan to confront the challenges Floridians faced. I said: "To tackle the big and relevant issues of our day with bold and innovative ideas is without question the most rewarding way to serve. What will it take to fully capitalize on the opportunities before us? It will take what it has always taken: leadership."

I believe that is true at every level of politics. And I believe that the measure of our politicians is not in how good they look on TV or how popular they are with the media; it's in their ideas to help everyday people: the single mom desperate to give her kids a better shot in life, the college graduate with crippling student debt and no job, the working parents struggling against a rising tide of bills and payments.

So before I became speaker, I toured the state to talk with people in difficult circumstances just like those, and I put together a book titled *100 Innovative Ideas for Florida's Future*. We conducted "idearaisers" throughout the state and created a Web site to invite Floridians to submit their own ideas. We came up with an agenda that included innovations like a requirement that school districts create career academies for vocational training, an investment pool for businesses and infrastructure projects, and a Web site that allows consumers to compare Florida doctors, hospitals and health insurance plans—these were just three ideas along with ninety-seven others. Through this book, Floridians knew exactly what my goals would be in office, and I stuck to those goals and am proud of what we achieved as a result.

This method of leadership—powered by ideas and sustained by an open communication of those ideas to the people they impact—is certainly not one that I invented myself. Others have taken a similar approach, often with great success. One of the most notable instances was an initiative announced twenty years ago last fall: the Contract with America.

The Contract with America was led by Representative Newt Gingrich of Georgia, then minority whip and future speaker of the House. He partnered with other Republican leaders, including Texas Congressman Dick Armey and policy leaders at the Heritage Foundation, to craft a revolutionary collection of ideas for restoring the promise of America. Every Republican candidate signed the contract—and that November, the American people gave it their stamp of approval by giving Republicans the majority in the U.S. Congress.

Today, the American Dream faces enormous challenges. These have been brought on by dramatic changes to the nature of our economy, and made worse by the failure of our policies and institutions to adapt. In the last elections, the voters made clear their dissatisfaction with the status quo. But we must do more—much more—than separate ourselves from the failed ideas of our current leaders. The temptation for Republicans after these elections will be to look for ways to keep the majority in 2016, to pursue small ideas that poll well but will do little to address the massive economic changes we are facing. But my hope is that we will use our new majority in the Senate and our larger majority in the House to offer and implement a twenty-first-century agenda to restore and expand the American Dream. After all, protest elections—even ones that (temporarily) benefit my party—will not save the American Dream.

Americans are anxious. The institutions that used to work—like our educational system—no longer work. The wages of the working class no longer keep pace with the modern cost of living. And so we veer back and forth with each election cycle, looking for the party that promises to take us back to the good old days. But the twentieth century is over, and it is never coming back. What we are facing now are massive structural economic changes, not just the aftermath of a cyclical downturn. And until we accept that, we won't get it right. Until we accept that we live in a world in which jobs, investment, talent, contagions and threats are no longer confined by national borders—that we have to restore American strength and leadership in order to restore the American Dream—no party will provide the solutions we seek. And until we understand that we need to move our economic, educational, health care, retirement and poverty-fighting institutions into the twenty-first century—not simply pour more money into them—we won't restore our hope and greatness.

The duty of Republicans who serve or aspire to serve in public office today is much as it was twenty-one years ago: We must stand for ideas that are modern, relevant, bold and innovative. Just as I did in the Florida House, I have spent this year developing the reform solutions described in this book. On some, I've partnered with leaders from both parties, such as Senators Mike Lee (Utah), Ron Wyden (Oregon), Chris Coons (Delaware) and Cory Booker (New Jersey), as well as Representatives Paul Ryan (Wisconsin) and Aaron Schock (Illinois). I've learned a great deal from the innovative conservative thinkers at the American Enterprise Institute. I've admired and borrowed liberally from the conservative reform ideas of Yuval Levin, Peter Wehner and others in *Room to Grow: Conservative Reforms for a Limited Government and a Thriving Middle Class*. There is an impressive number of conservative intellectuals and public policy experts coming up with ideas to save the American Dream today.

The proposals that I have developed with the help of other conservatives will reach all Americans, regardless of party. They will make higher education accessible to everyone, help struggling single mothers rise above poverty, spur the transformative innovation that can create new industries and millions of jobs, open America to the possibilities and realities of our increasingly globalized economy, save our crucial retirement programs from self-destruction and encourage rather than punish marriage and parenthood. I place no copyright on these ideas. I encourage and welcome any candidate for office today, in either party, to adopt these policies to their own platform—and, if elected, to help me improve them. Because I truly believe that despite our challenges, we Americans have good reason to be hopeful.

The most exciting moment in human history is upon us. And no nation is better positioned to access the full promise of the

twenty-first century than the United States. But first, we need
leaders who will offer hope and ideas—the hope of ushering in the
most prosperous era in human history, and the ideas required to
make it a reality. Our current administration and many of its allies
were elected by offering exactly that. They promised "hope" and
assured our people their ideas would move us "forward." They
have failed on both counts. Instead of hope and ideas, they have
clung to hopeless ideas. Instead of moving us forward, they have
moved us backward.

Yet despite this failure, most Democrats today are running on
the same stale and failed ideas. Instead of looking at the modern
needs of our people, they suggest pumping today's money into
yesterday's policies and programs, many of which have been failing for decades. They somehow believe that these programs are the
source of our jobs and prosperity. For proof, look no further than
Hillary Clinton's astonishing statement while campaigning in
Boston last fall. "Don't let anyone tell you it's businesses and corporations that create jobs," she said. Mrs. Clinton's statement
echoes the president's infamous declaration, "If you've got a business, you didn't build that."

There's no other way to put it: Both of these statements are just
wrong. They're wrong in economic terms, and they're wrong in
their assumptions about the American character. Government can
help—and government can certainly hinder—but it's the entrepreneurs, the strivers and the risk takers who create jobs. Government's role is to make our nation the easiest and best place in the
world to create those jobs. If we lose sight of that fact, we will have
driven the final nail in the coffin of the American Dream.

Not long ago, ours was still largely a national economy. But now the world is shrinking. And our economy is more connected and less insulated than ever before from events half a world away. As a result, today foreign policy *is* domestic policy. So much of what happens here at home is directly related to what happens abroad. When liberty and economic freedom spread, they create markets for our products, visitors to our tourist destinations, partners for our businesses, investors for our ideas and jobs for our people. But when liberty is denied and economic desperation takes root, it affects us here at home too. It breeds radicalism and terrorism, drives illegal immigration and leads to humanitarian crises we are compelled to address.

The same fluidity of global investment and talent, the same connections of people and ideas that are erasing the distinctions between life in America and events abroad, are also changing our wages, our jobs, the skills we need to succeed in the twenty-first century and the options of those with investment and talent to offer. Our great challenge—our unavoidable task if we are to remain a great nation—is to change our policies and our government to adapt to this changing world. It is no longer a question of if we will adapt, but how we will change: whether we will build a new American Century or consign ourselves to becoming merely one nation among many.

Because flickering on this shrinking globe is the promise of the American Dream. It was a bright flame when it attracted my parents to America. And even though it is guttering today, it still burns. This generation has the opportunity to ensure that the light of the American Dream animates the lives of all Americans for centuries to come.

Our assorted problems have left many feeling overwhelmed today and less confident about tomorrow. Yearning for a better time when our leaders had answers and our institutions worked. Yet there is no time in our history I would rather live in than right here, right now. For we are on the eve of a new American Century. The most prosperous and secure era in our nation's history is within our reach. All that is required of us is to do what those who came before us did: confront our challenges and embrace our opportunities. And when we do, we will leave for our children what our parents left for us: the most exceptional nation in all of human history.

—Senator Marco Rubio
November 2014

Epilogue

A LETTER FROM THE AUTHOR

I announced my campaign for president of the United States on April 13, 2015. At virtually every event I have attended since then, I have met someone or seen something that reminded me of my parents.

My mom and dad were both born to poor families in Cuba—a society like most in the world, where a person's future depended on who his or her parents were. After years of frustration and disappointment, they knew they wanted more for themselves. So in 1956, they came to America.

Their early years here were not easy. They arrived with no money and very little education, but in time found good jobs. My father worked his way up to being a bartender on Miami Beach and later in Las Vegas. My mother worked as a cashier, a maid, and a stock clerk at K-Mart. They eventually earned enough to buy a home, raise a family, and retire with security. Most important to them, they were able to leave their children better off than themselves.

My parents accomplished these things even though they were never wealthy. Just a few years removed from poverty and despair, they achieved a happy life. They achieved the American Dream.

As this campaign has gone on, I have regularly been reminded that I do not come from privilege. If "privilege" is defined as a childhood surrounded by wealth and power, then that is certainly true. My parents never made enough to pay for my education. In fact, I had over $100,000 in student loans that I finished paying off only in the last few years. I did not inherit any money or real estate, either. And I didn't have any family connections to help me land my first job out of law school or to bring in big checks for my first political campaign, which was for City Commissioner of my hometown of West Miami.

Yet I consider myself to be a child of incredible privilege, because I was raised in a stable home by two parents who loved each other and loved their children, and who taught me that no dream was too big and no goal out of reach—because I was an American.

My parents' life journey and the opportunities they provided for me were possible because they lived in America during the American century. The twentieth century is remembered as the American century because our nation led the world against evil multiple times and because our economy produced the best companies, the best products, and the best jobs in the world.

Nothing has changed about the greatness of our people, but the world is a fundamentally different place today than it was back then. For much of the twentieth century, America had limited international competition, but now we are engaged in a global competition for the best companies, talent, ideas, and jobs. We also had plenty of good paying work, even for people like my parents with a limited education, but now many jobs pay too little or are being replaced by machines. And while global affairs back then were defined by World Wars and also a cold one, now America faces a more diverse set of threats—from autocratic governments in China, Russia, and Iran to radical jihadists.

Today, we live in the most significant period of change since the industrial revolution. These changes have disrupted every aspect of our lives, and it is clear that the old way of doing things no longer works. In this new era, it is no longer enough to choose leaders based on what they claim to have achieved in the past. Now more than ever, we must choose our leaders based on what they understand about our future.

Millions of hardworking families live paycheck to paycheck, but the only answer our outdated leaders can come up with is the old idea of hiking taxes on the rich and raising the minimum wage by a few dollars. Millions of young Americans owe thousands in student loans for degrees that have not led to jobs, but the only answer our outdated leaders can come up with is to slightly lower monthly payments. On the global stage, China, Russia, and Iran increasingly dominate important regions; radical jihadists take cities once liberated at the price of American lives, stealing the weapons we left behind; and our allies no longer trust us. Yet our outdated leaders pursue a reset with Russia and a deal with Iran, slash military spending and weaken our intelligence programs, slander allies such as Israel, and refuse to call radical Islam by its name.

We live in a time unlike any before it, with problems and opportunities unique to this moment. I am running for president because we need leaders grounded in the future—leaders who think originally and bring to the table new, innovative ideas to confront the major challenges facing us in this century.

One of those challenges is that, while the cost of living keeps climbing, almost two-thirds of Americans make less money today than they did in 2002.[1] We cannot be a great country if millions of our people are permanently trapped living paycheck to paycheck. As we have seen, stale ideas from yesterday will not help us solve this problem. When I am president, we will put in place new ideas that help increase your paycheck and reduce your bills.

First, we will reform the tax and regulatory codes so that businesses are encouraged to raise wages. Under my tax reform plan, the more people a company hires and the more it pays its employees, the less that company will owe in taxes. We will also cap how much regulations can cost our economy so that businesses can direct their money into wage and job growth rather than lawyers and compliance costs. Just since 2008, federal regulations have cost our private sector $733.9 billion—money that could have gone into building businesses, creating jobs, and raising wages.[2]

Second, we will help those in low-paying jobs move to higher-paying jobs by transforming the way we provide higher education and skills training. Instead of pushing everyone to go to a traditional college, we will provide more opportunities to become welders, electricians, auto technicians, or plumbers, which are valuable and high-paying trades. We will also have flexible college programs that award degrees based on what you know, not how many hours you spend in a classroom. On the K–12 level, we will give education back to states, local school boards, and parents instead of leaving it to Washington bureaucrats in the Department of Education or to the one-size-fits-all Common Core curriculum standards.

Third, we will take steps to make life in America more affordable for working families. The simplest way to do this is to let working parents keep more of the money they earn by increasing the child tax credit. We must also take a few common-sense steps to once again lead the world in producing oil and natural gas, which will drive down electric bills and fuel expenses for our families.

These policy goals will help us confront the challenge of stagnant wages and a rising cost of living, but a second, related challenge still remains: our economy isn't growing fast enough to produce good jobs, which is leaving millions of Americans—particularly young Americans—unable to find work or start a business, stuck with crippling student loans, and on the verge of inheriting a massive national debt. Stale ideas from yesterday will not help us solve this problem, but when I am president, we will put in place policies that spark the innovation that will lead to exciting twenty-first-century jobs, make student loans easier to pay, and prevent the next generation from having to foot the bill for our outdated leaders' inability to restrain themselves.

First, we need growth and innovation policies that capture the potential of the new technologies our people are developing so that young people and all people can benefit from the jobs and wealth they will create. This will require, in part, making America the best place in the world to start your own business. We need to repeal the regulations that are killing the small banks that loan money to start-ups. We need to lower taxes for small businesses so they can compete with big businesses. And we must repeal and replace ObamaCare before it repeals and replaces more American jobs.

Second, we will help those struggling with student loans by allowing them to repay based on their income levels. For current and future students, we will require colleges to tell them how much they can expect to earn with their degrees before they take out the loans to pay for them.

Third, we will make sure that young Americans will not be forced to pay higher taxes down the road in order to cover our $18 trillion national debt. We will balance our budget through a combination of growth and spending reforms. We will also save Social Security and Medicare, which are currently on a path to bankrupt themselves and our nation. These vital programs must be saved in order to still exist when the next generation retires.

These policy goals will help us create jobs by growing our economy rather than our government, and they will bring millions of young Americans out from under the shadow of debt. But another challenge remains. We still have leaders who cling to the old idea that government is more important than family. The resulting erosion of our values and culture is limiting the futures of our children and causing massive economic and societal fallout. When I am president, we will have a government that strengthens the family rather than competes with it, and that encourages our values rather than attempts to replace them.

First, we will remove the penalties in our tax code and safety net programs that punish marriage. It is marriage—not government—that has the proven ability to reduce poverty and boost the futures of our children. Second, we will redesign our antipoverty system so it cures poverty through education, responsibility, and work. Third, I will appoint judges and an attorney general who will protect our Second Amendment rights and defend those who hold traditional values from discrimination or harassment.

The final fundamental challenge we face is the danger caused by leaders who assume America can no longer afford to be the most powerful nation on earth. In recent years, America's influence has declined, the world has grown more dangerous, and our people and interests have become less secure. When I am president, we will be trusted by our allies, feared by our enemies, and respected by all.

First, we will end the dangerous cuts to our military. Second, we will have a strategy to deal with threats to our security and prosperity posed by China, Russia, Iran, and radical Islam. Third, we will have a foreign policy with moral clarity that supports those who pursue peace, democracy, and respect for human rights. When I am president, there will be no doubt that America will do whatever it takes to help Israel prosper as a Jewish state.

A strong America, with strong values, good jobs, and a healthy economy—this is the future that is within our reach. The twenty-first century can be the greatest chapter ever in the story of America, but it will require new leaders with new ideas for a new era.

While we should always be proud of our history, our work must be about tomorrow.

Those who want to remain in power will always resist the transition to a new generation of leadership. Like many younger candidates for office, I often hear from those who say it isn't my turn. They said the same thing in 2009 when I ran for Senate against the then-sitting Republican governor. The entire Party establishment in Washington and Florida told me I had no chance. In fact, the only people who thought I could win all lived in my home . . . and four of them were under the age of ten! What these critics do not understand is that for America, the future is now. The twenty-first century will not slow down and wait for us, and if we keep promoting the same leaders, we will be left behind.

I also hear from those who say, patronizingly, that now is not my time but that I have "a bright future." That is good news, because this election is about the future. In fact, I argue that it is already taking place in the future! Once again, these comments are nothing new. When I ran for speaker of the Florida House, I heard many of the same statements over and over. But I tuned out these politicians and listened instead to the people of our state. I gathered together their ideas and wrote a book titled *100 Innovative Ideas for Florida's Future*, which went on to drive my time as speaker. Many of the ideas in it became law, and I'm proud to say that—even while facing a real estate crisis we inherited and a hostile governor and Senate—we balanced our budget without raising taxes and improved our public schools without a Common Core.

Another criticism has also arisen, and this one *is* new. Some now tell me that I am not rich enough to be president, as if a person's bank account says something about his ability to serve his nation. While it is true that we are not wealthy, Jeanette and I still consider our family extremely blessed. We have been able to pay off student loans, send our children to Christian schools, and invest in their futures by saving for college. We also make sure we set a portion of money aside to donate to charity, because we believe God calls us to share our blessings with others. And on the fifth of every month, we usually have just enough left to pay the only significant debt we have left: the mortgage on our family home.

Despite this mortgage, the biggest debt I have will never be to a bank. The biggest debt I have will always be to America—for this is not just the nation I was born in, it is the nation that changed the history of my family.

My father lost his mother when he was nine years old. He had to leave school and go to work. He would work for the next seventy years of his life. When he was young he had big dreams, but they became impossible to achieve. Giving his children the chance to do all the things he never could became the purpose of his life. For years, he worked as a banquet bartender on nights, weekends, and even holidays, and well into his seventies.

He was grateful for the work he had, but it was not the life he wanted for his children. My father stood behind a small portable bar in the back of a room for all those years so that one day I could stand behind a podium in the front of a room. That journey, from behind the bar to behind a podium, is the essence of the American Dream.

This is not my story alone. It is our story. We are all but a generation or two removed from someone who made our futures the purpose of their lives. Whether we remain a special country will depend on whether that journey is still possible for those trying to make it now. That is why this election is not just about what laws we will pass—it is a generational choice about what kind of country we will be.

It is a choice Americans before us were also called to make. At the turn of the nineteenth century, industrialization was transforming the world, but that generation of Americans left yesterday behind, harnessed the power of the industrial age, and the twentieth century became the American Century.

At midpoint of the twentieth century, Americans feared they were falling behind to the Soviet Union in space and on the global stage, but that generation turned the page on the past and pursued a New Frontier.

Now our own generation must choose what kind of country we want to be in this new century. Globalization and massive technological change present us with both great challenges and great opportunities. Like those before us, we must either embrace the future or be left behind by it. Our children will be either the first generation of Americans to inherit a diminished country or they will be the freest and most prosperous generation ever.

Americans not yet born will write the final verdict on our generation. Let them record that we made the right choice. Let them record that in the early years of this century, faced with a rapidly changing and uncertain world, our generation rose to face the great challenges of our time. Let them record that we preserved the one place in the world where who you come from does not determine how far you can go. Let them record that we ensured the American miracle lived on, and that because we did, our children and theirs lived in a new American Century.

—Senator Marco Rubio
June 2015

Acknowledgments

First and foremost, I thank my Lord, Jesus Christ, whose willingness to suffer and die for my sins will allow me to enjoy eternal life.

One of the things I've learned from writing two books is that they only come together through the hard work and dedication of many talented individuals. I'd like to thank the people in this book who shared their hopes and their struggles in their pursuit of the American Dream.

Once again, I was fortunate to have my very wise lawyer, Bob Barnett, and the outstanding team at Sentinel handling the publication of *American Dreams*. Thanks to Adrian Zackheim; Kary Perez; and especially to Niki Papadopoulos, who provided invaluable edits to the manuscript. I am grateful to Jessica Gavora for helping me craft and organize the manuscript, interview the people who shared their life stories and meet the various deadlines on time.

Thanks to the many scholars and policy experts whose writings, ideas and advice have helped shape my views on both domestic and foreign policy. The American Enterprise Institute (AEI), in particular, has been a tremendous resource to me. I am grateful to its president, Arthur Brooks, and its stable of talented scholars, including James Pethokoukis, Andrew Biggs, Alan D. Viard, Andrew Kelly, Robert Doar, W. Bradford Wilcox, Michael Strain, Jeffrey Eisenach and Mark Schneider.

I am also immensely indebted to the intellectual leaders of the "reform conservative" movement—Yuval Levin, Reihan Salam, Ross Douthat, Ramesh Ponnuru, and several of the above mentioned AEI scholars—whose innovative ideas are moving conservatism into the twenty-first century. I am also grateful to a number of policy experts for their creative ideas on welfare, health care, retirement security, tax and regulatory reform and higher education, including Oren Cass, Ron Haskins, Stuart Butler, Scott Winship, Jim Capretta, Chuck Blahous, Jason Fichtner, Glenn Hubbard, Doug Holtz-Eakin, Peter Wehner, Bob Stein, Marc Sumerlin, Andy Laperriere, former Senator Phil Gramm, David Burton, Stephen Moore, Bob Carroll, William McBride, Stephen Entin, Jason Delisle, Nina Rees, Neal McCluskey, George Leef and Richard Vedder. On national security and foreign policy, I am thankful for the wise advice and counsel from Elliott Abrams, Bob Kagan, Eric Edelman, James Carafano, Brian Hook, former Senator Jim Talent and Pete Hegseth.

Many thanks to the talented individuals on my Senate staff who helped me develop the legislative proposals I write about in this book: Cesar Conda, Sally Canfield, Scott Parkinson, Emily Bouck, J. R. Sanchez, Darren Achord, Sara Decker, Jon Baselice,

Jamie Fly, Brian Walsh, Victor Cervino, Enrique Gonzalez and Gregg Nunziata. I am also grateful to Rob Noel, Todd Reid and Jessica Fernandez. Thanks to Heath Thompson, Todd Harris, Alberto Martinez, Alex Conant and Alex Burgos for their valuable comments on the manuscript.

I am indebted to my colleagues Senator Mike Lee of Utah, Representative Paul Ryan of Wisconsin, Senator Ron Wyden of Oregon, Senator Chris Coons of Delaware, Senator Mark Warner of Virginia, Senator Tim Scott of South Carolina and Senator Cory Booker of New Jersey for partnering with me on many of the legislative proposals I mention in this book. I am confident that we will eventually turn these solutions into realities.

Thanks to Norman Braman, not only for the advice and comments on the book, but for your friendship and wise advice to me over the years.

As ever, I am grateful to my family—Jeanette, my wife, and our children, Amanda, Daniella, Anthony and Dominick—for their continued love, understanding and support.

Notes

CHAPTER ONE

1. Scott Winship, "Our Misleading Obsession with Growth Rates," *Breakthrough Journal*, Winter 2013.
2. "The Lost Decade of the Middle Class," Pew Research Social & Demographic Trends, August 22, 2012.
3. "The Low-Wage Recovery and Growing Inequality," National Employment Law Project, August 2012.
4. Tyler Cowen, *Average Is Over: Powering America Beyond the Age of the Great Stagnation* (New York: Dutton, 2013), p. 38.
5. "The Number of Jobs Grows, but Not Labor Force Participation," *Washington Post*, June 6, 2014.
6. Nicholas Eberstadt, "America's Increasingly Irrelevant 'Unemployment Rate,'" RealClearMarkets.com, May 14, 2014.
7. OECD Skills Outlook 2013.
8. W. Bradford Wilcox, "Marriage Makes Our Children Richer—Here's Why," *The Atlantic*, October 29, 2013.
9. Ron Haskins, "Getting Ahead in America," *National Affairs*, Fall 2009.

10. Ron Haskins and Isabel Sawhill, *Creating an Opportunity Society* (Washington D.C.: Brookings Institution Press, 2009).

11. Eric Morath, "Who Benefits from a Higher Minimum Wage?," *Wall Street Journal*, February 12, 2014.

CHAPTER TWO

1. Joshua Green, "The Incredible Stair-Climbing, Self-Parking, Amphibious Wheelchair," *Bloomberg Businessweek*, June 5, 2014.

2. "Not Open for Business," *The Economist*, October 12, 2013.

3. Ben Goad and Julian Hattem, "Regulation Nation: Obama Oversees Expansion of the Regulatory State," *The Hill*, August 19, 2013.

4. "Not Open for Business," *The Economist*, October 12, 2013.

5. Tim Devaney, "Obama Regs Have Cost $500B, Report Finds," *The Hill*, January 8, 2014.

6. Avik Roy, "Marco Rubio's Important New Proposal for Containing the Costs of Federal Regulation," *Forbes*, March 10, 2014.

7. Grant Smith, "U.S. Seen as Biggest Oil Producer After Overtaking Saudi Arabia," Bloomberg, July 4, 2014.

8. Edward L. Morse, "Welcome to the Revolution," *Foreign Affairs*, May/June 2014.

CHAPTER THREE

1. "The War on Poverty: 50 Years Later," House Budget Committee Report, March 3, 2014.

2. Ibid.

3. Hope Yen, "Nation's Poor at 49.7M, Higher Than Official Rate," Associated Press, November 6, 2013.

4. James Pethokoukis, "70 Percent of Americans Born at the Bottom Never Reach the Middle," American Enterprise Institute, July 18, 2014.

5. James Pethokoukis, "The U.S. Can Have More Economic Mobility Than Canada, Right?," American Enterprise Institute, August 15, 2013.

6. Keith Hall, Testimony Before the Senate Budget Committee, April 1, 2014.

7. Ibid.

8. "Rural Poverty and Well-Being," United States Department of Agriculture Economic Research Service, February 28, 2014.

9. "Broke in the 'Burbs," *The Economist*, July 20, 2013.

10. Ibid.

11. "Making Work Search Smart—Utah, 2013," NextJob.

12. "Making Work Search Smart—Mississippi, 2013," NextJob.

13. OECD Employment Outlook 2005.

14. Jake Grovum, "States Resist Food Stamp Cuts," *Stateline*, Pew Charitable Trusts, March 17, 2014.

15. Robert Doar, "Ten Welfare-Reform Lessons," *National Review*, April 14, 2014.

16. "The War on Poverty: 50 Years Later," House Budget Committee Report, March 3, 2014.

CHAPTER FOUR

1. "The Rising Cost of Not Going to College," Pew Research Social & Demographic Trends, February 11, 2014.

2. Sophie Quinton and Stephanie Stamm, "What Happened to the High School Class of 2004?" *National Journal*, January 27, 2014.

3. "The Rising Cost of Not Going to College," Pew Research Social & Demographic Trends, February 11, 2014.

4. Ibid.

5. Ron Haskins, "Getting Ahead in America," *National Affairs*, Fall 2009.

6. Andrew Kelly, "Why Conservatives Should Crack the College Conundrum," *Forbes*, March 26, 2014.

7. Richard Vedder and Christopher Denhart, "How the College Bubble Will Pop," *Wall Street Journal*, January 8, 2014.

8. "Tuition and Fee and Room and Board Charges Over Time, 173–74 Through 2013–14, Selected Years," College Board, Trends in Higher Education, 2014.

9. Stuart M. Butler, "The Coming Higher-Ed Revolution," *National Affairs*, Winter 2012.

10. "Fact Sheet on the President's Plan to Make College More Affordable: A Better Bargain for the Middle Class," WhiteHouse.gov, August 22, 2013.

11. Stuart M. Butler, "The Coming Higher-Ed Revolution," *National Affairs*, Winter 2012.

12. Phil Izzo, "Congratulations to the Class of 2014, Most Indebted Ever," *Wall Street Journal*, May 16, 2014.

13. Sam Frizell, "Student Loans Are Ruining Your Life. Now They're Ruining the Economy Too," *Time*, February 26, 2014.

14. Phil Izzo, "Congratulations to the Class of 2014, Most Indebted Ever," *Wall Street Journal*, May 16, 2014.

15. Jon Marcus, "New Analysis Shows Problematic Boom in Higher Ed Administrators," New England Center for Investigative Reporting, February 6, 2014.

16. Andrew Martin, "Building a Showcase Campus, Using an I.O.U.," *New York Times*, December 13, 2012.

17. "Consumer Credit—G.19," Board of Governors of the Federal Reserve System, May 7, 2014.

18. Phyllis Korkki, "The Ripple Effects of Rising Student Debt," *New York Times*, May 24, 2014.

19. Meta Brown and Sydnee Caldwell, "Young Student Loan Borrowers Retreat from Housing and Auto Markets," Liberty Street Economics, NY Fed blog, April 17, 2013.

20. Neil Irwin, "Why the Housing Market Is Still Stalling the Economy," *New York Times*, April 24, 2014.

21. Richard Kim, "The Audacity of Occupy Wall Street," *The Nation*, November 21, 2011.

22. Anthony P. Carnevale and Ban Cheah, "Hard Times: College Majors, Unemployment and Earnings," Georgetown Public Policy Institute, Center on Education and the Workforce, Georgetown University, 2013.

23. Dan Alexander, "Big Business Bets on Education, Turning Factories and Corporate Campuses into Schools," *Forbes*, December 9, 2013.

24. Matthew Philips, "Welders, America Needs You," *Bloomberg Businessweek*, March 20, 2014.

25. "Higher Ed's Illusions," *Wall Street Journal*, February 27, 2014.

26. Andrew Kelly, "Tomorrow's Online Schools," *National Review*, October 28, 2013.

27. Ibid.

28. Devon Haynie, "Online Education Isn't Always Cheap," *U.S. News & World Report*, August 28, 2013.

CHAPTER FIVE

1. See the graphic for yourself here: www.census.gov/dataviz/visualizations/019/.

2. Derek Thompson, "Map: The Astonishing Concentration of High-Income Earners Around Washington, D.C.," *The Atlantic*, December 17, 2013.

3. James Pethokoukis, "A Reply to the *Wall Street Journal*'s Kim Strassel on Taxes and Reform Conservatism," American Enterprise Institute, June 25, 2014.

4. *Room to Grow: Conservative Reforms for a Limited Government and a Thriving Middle Class*, YGNetwork.org.

5. Barack Obama, "Remarks by the President to a Joint Session of Congress on Health Care," Washington D.C., September 9, 2009, www.whitehouse.gov/the_press_office/Remarks-by-the-President-to-a-Joint-Session-of-Congress-on-Health-Care.

6. Louise Radnofsky, "Premiums Rise at Big Insurers, Fall at Small Rivals Under Health Law," *Wall Street Journal*, June 18, 2014.

7. Ken Alltucker, "Health Net to Raise Affordable Care Act Rates by Nearly 14 Percent," *Arizona Republic*, June 17, 2014.

8. Ben Sutherly, "Obamacare Premiums to Rise 13 Percent, Ohio Agency Says," *Columbus Dispatch*, May 30, 2014.

9. Byron York, "Why Obamacare 'Good News' Applies Only to the Poor," *Washington Examiner*, June 19, 2014.

10. Ibid.

11. "The Budget and Economic Outlook: 2014 to 2024," Congressional Budget Office, February 4, 2014.

12. Lyndsey Layton, "In New Orleans, Major School District Closes Traditional Public Schools for Good," *Washington Post*, May 28, 2014.

CHAPTER SIX

1. Angela Johnson, "76% of Americans Are Living Paycheck-to-Paycheck," CNN Money, June 24, 2013.

2. Nancy Hellmich, "Retirement: A Third Have Less Than $1,000 Put Away," *USA Today*, April 1, 2014.

3. Nari Rhee, "Race and Retirement Insecurity in the United States," National Institute on Retirement Security, December 2013.

4. Jeanne Meister, "Job Hopping Is the 'New Normal' for Millennials: Three Ways to Prevent a Human Resource Nightmare," *Forbes*, August 14, 2012.

5. David C. John, "Pursuing Universal Retirement Security Through Automatic IRAs and Account Simplification," Testimony to the House Committee on Ways and Means, April 17, 2012.

6. "Retirement Statistics," Statistic Brain, January 1, 2014.

7. "Merrill Lynch Study Finds 72 Percent of People Over the Age of 50 Want to Work in Retirement," *Wall Street Journal*, June 4, 2014.

8. I recommend this comprehensive treatment of Social Security reform

by Andrew Biggs of the American Enterprise Institute: Andrew G. Biggs, "A New Vision for Social Security," *National Affairs*, Summer 2013.

9. Ibid.

10. Ibid.

11. "Life Expectancy for Social Security," Social Security Administration.

12. "CMS Office of the Actuary Projects Modest Health Spending Growth," Centers for Medicare and Medicaid Services, September 18, 2013.

13. "Survey: Medicare Prescription Drug Benefit Earns High Marks 10 Years After Enactment," Medicare Today, September 17, 2013.

14. "Paul Ryan's Medicare Voucher Plan Improves with Each Pass," Bloomberg, March 20, 2012.

CHAPTER SEVEN

1. Ron Haskins, "Marriage, Parenthood, and Public Policy," *National Affairs*, Spring 2014.

2. Isabel V. Sawhill, "How Marriage and Divorce Impact Economic Opportunity," Brookings Institute, May 6, 2014.

3. Raj Chetty, Nathaniel Hendren, Patrick Kline and Emmanuel Saez, "Where Is the Land of Opportunity? The Geography of Intergenerational Mobility in the U.S.," National Bureau of Economic Research, Working Paper 19843, January 2014.

4. James Pethokoukis, "Why Intact Families Are Key to Shared American Prosperity," American Enterprise Institute, June 25, 2014.

5. James Pethokoukis, "Can Anything Really Be Done About Family Breakdown and American Poverty? A Q&A with Brad Wilcox," American Enterprise Institute, March 11, 2014.

6. Robert Maranto and Michael Crouch, "Ignoring an Inequality Culprit: Single-Parent Families," *Wall Street Journal*, April 20, 2014.

7. Robert Doar, "Back to Work: How to Improve the Prospects of Low-

Income Americans," Statement Before the U.S. Senate Committee on the Budget, February 25, 2014.

8. Alia Malek, "Dead Broke, Not Deadbeat: Baltimore Rethinks Welfare Policy," Al Jazeera America, January 15, 2014.

9. Annie Lowrey, "MTV's '16 and Pregnant,' Derided by Some, May Resonate as a Cautionary Tale," *New York Times*, January 13, 2014.

EPILOGUE

1. Jim Tankersley, "The 21st Century Has Been Terrible for Working Americans," *Washington Post*, March 6, 2015.

2. Ben Gitis and Sam Batkins, "Regulatory Impact on Small Business Establishments," *American Action Forum*, April 24, 2015.

Index